D1807598

"We're living through a frantic and feverish time in history, and simultaneously in a golden age of playwriting. The fastest society is colliding with the slowest art form. This book will guide you to the center of that collision, where you can locate the love and ferocity that draws you to writing while sharpening your craft and getting your play on to the stage."

Rob Handel, *Chair of Dramatic Writing, Carnegie Mellon University*

"*Playwriting with Purpose* is an empowering and accessible playwriting companion for new and experienced writers alike. Goldfinger draws on an exceptionally wide range of classical and contemporary texts from around the globe to create an expansive and inspiring provocation of what a play can be. I love that this book considers both the art and the artist – encouraging playwrights to think about *why* and *how* they write, as well as what they write. It demystifies and offers practical advice on navigating the business of playwriting – from writing applications to networking – offering valuable insight into the inner workings of an industry that is often overwhelming to new playwrights. This engaging, encouraging and comprehensive guide to both the craft and business of playwriting feels like having your own personal mentor in your pocket!"

Dr Jenny Knotts, *PhD in Playwriting, University of Glasgow*

"I wish I had this book when I began my writing journey. It's fresh, funny, thought-provoking, and provides important insights into the industry so that playwrights can get their work on stage immediately."

Antoinette Nwandu, *Award-Winning Playwright and Screenwriter, Broadway and Netflix*

Playwriting with Purpose

Playwriting with Purpose: A Guide and Workbook for New Playwrights, Second Edition provides a revised and greatly expanded holistic approach to playwriting from an award-winning playwright and professor.

This book incorporates craft lessons, scenes for study, and concrete guidance in both the art and business of playwriting. The author takes readers through the entire creative process, from creating characters and writing dialogue to revising and producing your play. Each chapter includes incisive craft lessons, provocative writing exercises and prompts, examples from plays, tips from working artists, reading recommendations, and more. Thoroughly revised, new features to this edition include:

- Vastly expanded sections on structure, world building, business of playwriting, writing for television and film, and more.
- New writing exercises and pro tips from working playwrights in each chapter.
- An exploration of art and craft through a new selection of international plays.
- Shorter chapters with more subject headings to make it easier to find the exact craft lesson or writing prompt you want when you want it.

Playwriting with Purpose gives writers and students the tools to succeed in today's theater industry.

Jacqueline Goldfinger is an award-winning playwright, dramaturg, and librettist. Her work has been produced around the world, including performances at The Kennedy Center,

Sydney Opera House, Contemporary American Theatre Festival, École nationale de théâtre du Canada, and BBC Radio 3, among others. As an educator, she has taught playwriting and dramaturgy at the University of Pennsylvania (undergraduate), University of California, Davis (graduate), and others. She was the Guest Editor for the new play issue of the *Journal of American Drama and Theatre*. As a dramaturg, she has worked on new plays at La Jolla Playhouse, Philadelphia Theatre Company, and others. For more information, visit www.jacquelinegoldfinger.com.

Playwriting with Purpose

A Guide and Workbook for Playwrights

Revised and Expanded Second Edition

Jacqueline Goldfinger

Routledge
Taylor & Francis Group

NEW YORK AND LONDON

Designed cover image: *Babel* at Theatre Exile, performers Bi Jean Ngo and Frank Nardi, photo by Paola Nogueras.

Second edition published 2025
by Routledge
605 Third Avenue, New York, NY 10158

and by Routledge
4 Park Square, Milton Park, Abingdon, Oxon, OX14 4RN

Routledge is an imprint of the Taylor & Francis Group, an informa business

First edition published by Routledge 2022

Library of Congress Cataloging-in-Publication Data
Names: Goldfinger, Jacqueline, author.
Title: Playwriting with purpose : a guide and workbook for playwrights / Jacqueline Goldfinger.
Description: Second edition. | New York, NY : Routledge, 2025. | Includes bibliographical references and index.
Identifiers: LCCN 2025001411 (print) | LCCN 2025001412 (ebook) | ISBN 9781032825960 (hardback) | ISBN 9781032825908 (paperback) | ISBN 9781003505310 (ebook)
Subjects: LCSH: Playwriting. | Drama—Technique.
Classification: LCC PN1661 .G64 2025 (print) | LCC PN1661 (ebook) | DDC 808.2—dc23/eng/20250117
LC record available at https://lccn.loc.gov/2025001411
LC ebook record available at https://lccn.loc.gov/2025001412

ISBN: 978-1-032-82596-0 (hbk)
ISBN: 978-1-032-82590-8 (pbk)
ISBN: 978-1-003-50531-0 (ebk)

DOI: 10.4324/9781003505310

Typeset in Stempel Garamond LT Pro
by Apex CoVantage, LLC

Each of us is a collection of stories.
Stories the world has told us.
Stories our family has told us.
Stories our religion has told us.
Stories our friends have told us.
Stories we have told ourselves.
If we change the stories, then we change ourselves.
If we change ourselves, then we change the world.
– Jacqueline Goldfinger

Contents

Playwrights Cited

- Kneubuhl, Victoria Nalani
- Kushner, Tony
- Lee, Kristine Haruna
- Lee, Young Jean
- Letts, Tracey
- Lorca, Frederico García
- Lynett, Rachel
- Lyons, Douglas
- McCraney, Terell Alvin
- McDonagh, Martin
- McPherson, Connor
- Maisel, Jennifer
- Mallén, Ana Caro de
- Mamet, David
- Majok, Martyna
- Marlowe, Christopher
- Mee, Charles
- Meyenburg, Marius von
- Millay, Edna St. Vincent
- Miller, Arthur
- Moench, Anna Ouyang
- Molière
- Moreno-Penson, Desi
- Morriseau, Dominique
- Nguyen, Qui
- Nottage, Lynn
- Nwandu, Antoinette
- O'Brien, Dan
- O'Hara, Robert
- O'Neill, Eugene
- Osmundsen, Dave
- Palmquist, Tina
- Parks, Suzan-Lori
- Ping, Chin Woon
- Pinter, Harold
- Pirandello, Luigi
- Polak, Brian James
- Pospisil, Craig
- Quintana, C.
- Raffo, Heather
- Reynoso, Mabelle
- Reza, Yasmina
- Rice, Tori
- Rivera, Jose
- Rogers, J.T.
- Romero, Elaine
- Ruhl, Sarah
- Saracho, Tanya
- Sayet, Madeline
- Schatz, Matt
- Schiller, Friedrich
- Schnitzler, Arthur
- Schwend, Emily
- Shaffer, Peter
- Shakespeare, William
- Shange, Ntozake
- Shawn, Wallace
- Shekar, Madhuri

- Shepard, Sam
- Sheridan, Richard Brinsley
- Shields, Erin
- Shifu, Wang
- Shōzō, Nakimi
- Sigurjónsson, Jóhann
- Silverman, Jen
- Smith, Anna Deavere
- Smith, Stef
- Solis, Octavio
- Son, Diana
- Song, Celine
- Sophocles
- Sorkin, Aaron
- Soyinka, Wole
- Spallen, Abbie
- Squire, Aurin
- Stephens, Simon
- Stoppard, Tom
- Strindberg, August
- Suh, Lloyd
- Sutherland, Efua
- Svich, Caridad
- Szymkowicz, Adam
- Tagore, Rabindranath
- Tarker, Kate
- Thomas, R. Eric
- Thompson, Lisa B.
- Tong, You
- Toossi, Sanaz
- Treadwell, Sophie
- Tremblay, Michel
- Tyrfingsson, Tyfingur
- Udofia, Mfoniso
- Urban, Ken
- Usigli, Rodolfo
- Vega, Lope de
- Vogel, Paula
- Walsh, Enda
- White, David Lee
- Wilde, Oscar
- Williams, Tennessee
- Wilson, August
- Wilder, Elyzabeth
- Wright, Doug
- Yehoshua, A.B.
- Yamauchi, Wakako
- Yee, Lauren

Groups Cited

- Cornerstone Theater Company
- National Theatre of the Deaf Ensemble
- The Neo-Futurists
- Noh.com/www.the-noh.com/ team
- Rainpan 43
- Tectonic Theatre Project

Artistic Advisors and Special Thanks

Senior Artistic Advisor
Dr. David S. Thompson
Annie Louise Harrison Waterman Professor Emeritus
of Theatre
Agnes Scott College

Artistic Advisors
Jessica Bashline, Curriculum Consultant
Quinn D. Eli, Community College of Philadelphia
Martine Kei Green-Rogers, DePaul University
Daniela Naranjo-Zarate, Theatremaker
Jeffrey Neuman, Playwright
Alix Rosenfeld, Dramaturg
Jerry Ruiz, Arizona State University
Edward Sobel, Villanova University
Stephanie Kyung Sun Walters, Friends Select School

Special Thanks
Lucia Accorsi
Promoth Jaikishan M
Alison Macfarlane
Stacey Walker
Drama Book Shop
Philadelphia Free Library

Introduction

How This Works

As you journey through this book, you will get a sense of the vast beauty and complexity of the theatre, which can hold all things, as it has for thousands of years. This book supports the creative journey of writers of all experience levels. You can work through the book from beginning to end to write a full play or skip around the book to focus on individual craft skills. Use this as a companion for your writing journey now and for years to come. The most important lesson I can impart is: You Can Write. You do not need anyone's permission to do so. If you write plays, then you are a playwright. Welcome to the party.

What is "Playwriting with Purpose"?

There is a myth that a play springs from a single thunderbolt of inspiration and immediately becomes a fully formed work of art. That is untrue. Even if a playwright is inspired, they must do the work to get the text onto the page. We all have work to do. We all have Purpose. That Purpose might feel easier at some moments, harder at others. But it is ever-present, and it binds us together – over days, years, decades, and centuries – so you're sitting with Kālidāsa and Kushner, Shange and Shakespeare, you and me.

DOI: 10.4324/9781003505310-1   1

"All the World's A Stage"[1]

"All the world's a stage." Literally. A stage can be a Broadway theatre or your living room, an open field, or an old factory. Theatre is shared in many ways, forms, and venues. When we say "stage," interpret that term broadly.

On a stage, you see performances. Performances are usually based on a "play" or "playscript," which is a text specifically written to be performed onstage. Plays contain dramatic elements like the dialogue spoken between performers*.

In the U.S., plays are often written by one person who shares their play with others after it is written. However, there are many ways to make plays, including having multiple writers or working with a group of artists to generate a performance, which is then written down as a playscript.

Overview

Theatre can be made in many ways and performed anywhere. A play is a text specifically written to be performed.

Reading Recommendations

The reading recommendations in this book are for educational purposes; they are *not* a "best-of" list. Students ask, "Why not use a best-of list?" and that's because there is no "best-of" list for art; that's one of the reasons art is endlessly alluring. Everyone has personal favorites based on their own metrics, backgrounds, and preferences.

For the purpose of my workshops, I select great plays based on the craft elements I want to illuminate for students. We discuss how and why the craft element works within the play. If a student is excited by a play, I recommend they read more work by that playwright. If not, learn the craft element and move on. Find what excites you and dive into those plays.

Overview

Focus on learning the craft lesson associated with the play, not whether you like the play itself.

Learning Goals for Teachers

This book is based on a series of workshops I taught at colleges and universities, community centers and theatres around the United States with these goals:

- Learn and practice the dramatic tools employed by playwrights.

- Be asked to think about performance broadly in terms of content, staging, and other elements of theatricality.
- Gain exposure to and engage with the voices of many different artists from around the world with varying points of view, ways of making, and voice.
- Explore the fundamentals of storytelling, character, and why something is engaging (or not) in live performance. Those fundamentals empower all theatre artists and audiences to engage with the work and the world in deeper and more nuanced ways.

Overview

Artists and audiences both benefit from understanding the fundamentals of theatre creation.

A Note to Students

Before we begin in earnest, let's discuss **The Overwhelming**. The Overwhelming is when students have writer's block because they are so overwhelmed by all the choices art asks us to make – all the rules we can live by or break.

I'm going to give you a lot of information. I'm going to share many ways that writers approach the same question; sometimes, these approaches will conflict with one another. Art is as finicky and joyous, complicated and confusing as life. So, make your artistic choices with confidence, keeping in mind that you can always go back and make a different choice later.

Some students worry that if they study the work of other artists, then their own writing will be less original (because they might borrow ideas or concepts from other writers). Do not worry. Your work is going to be uniquely you. We'll discuss this more in future chapters, but what's important at this moment is to know that you will be a stronger artist if you read, see, and engage with the work of other artists. There is a popular anecdote about playwright Tennessee Williams typing out all of Shakespeare's plays to understand storytelling better. I don't know if it's true, but I love the story.

Overview

If you get overwhelmed, just write. Make big choices. You can always revise in the future. Do not steal work, but know that similar stories told by different artists come out differently due to your unique perspective.

Now, let's write!

Resources
Additional Resource

- Playwrights on how they approach their writing process: https://youtu.be/VQ33WuaOhn8?si=GD MSdvPGUt2wsiIZ (National Theatre/London)

Note
1   A quote from William Shakespeare's *As You Like It.*

Writing Warm-Ups

Just like you stretch your body to prepare for an athletic tournament, you stretch your mind to prepare to write creatively. Sometimes, you need to stretch every day, and sometimes, only on special occasions. Regardless, use writing prompts to help you transition into your writing time and/or to work out your creative muscles so you become a stronger artist.

Writing Prompts

Playwright Suzan-Lori Parks of *Topdog/Underdog* says: "The writer has two kinds of faith: actual writing and sitting openly. Have faith in your personal effort or sweat. And faith in God, or whatever you want to call it. Then the voices will come. Faith is the big deal."[1]

Approach these writing prompts with faith. Just like any other skill, one-third of writing is innate talent, one-third is practice, and one-third is patience and time.

To participate in the following prompts, you'll need to know a few vocabulary words: Characters*, Dialogue*, Monologue*, Scene*, and Stage Directions*. If you do not know these terms, see the Glossary at the end of the book.

DOI: 10.4324/9781003505310-2

As you're work through the book, if you encounter theatre terms you do not know, then check out the Glossary. **The Glossary terms are starred (*) the first time it appears in the book.**

Overview

Dive into writing and have faith in yourself. If you encounter theatre terms you do not know, then see the Glossary at the end of the book.

Writing Prompt: Lists

This exercise helps generate material in a short period of time. Don't think about the prompts; simply respond to them by writing lists.

- For two minutes, write a list of objects in your purse/bag/pockets (i.e., keys, pen cap).
- For two minutes, write a list of places you hate (i.e., Halloween parties, dog houses).
- For two minutes, write a list of names that you love (i.e., José, Yetunde).
- For two minutes, write a list of lies you have told (i.e., I didn't eat your sandwich or sleep with your sister).
- For two minutes, write a list of your favorite things (i.e., wedding ring, paper crane).
- For two minutes, write a list of situations that make you want to punch someone (i.e., being told to smile, split infinitives).

- For two minutes, look over the lists and circle the words that excite you the most (even if you don't understand why they excite you). Put the full list aside in case you want it in the future. For the words you circled, write each of them on a sheet of paper. Fold those sheets of paper into smaller pieces and toss them into an empty cup. Leave the cup at the edge of your desk.

Now, you have a cauldron of bubbling ideas with some connection to your conscious and subconscious. Whenever you're stuck or just want some inspiration, draw a piece of paper and add the element to the scene you're writing. The element you include in your scene – objects from purses, favorite things, hated places – may or may not make it into any final draft, but they give you a quick springboard into writing with a prompt that is both unexpected yet connected to you.

Overview

Get stuck? Randomly select one of the pieces of paper from the previous exercise and write!

Writing Prompts: Short Prompts

In what follows, you'll find prompts that you can easily use to write for ten minutes, 30 minutes, or an hour. These are flexible; there is no way to do them incorrectly. Just write.

- Write a scene where a young child tries to drive a car.
- Write a scene at a lake house where one sibling wants to swim, but the other is afraid of the water.
- Write a scene in which a cat is trying to lure a bird down from the safety of a high branch.
- Write a monologue where a patient complains to a doctor because they do not want to take their medicine. Instead, the patient thinks doing something silly (like swimming with a zebra) will heal them.
- Write a scene that ends with a wedding. Now, use the same characters, but write a scene that ends with a funeral.
- Write a monologue from the point of view of a rockstar on a poster in your teenage bedroom.
- Write a scene where your character moves between different time periods.
- Write a scene between two siblings who both want Grandma's wedding ring. It holds an important, but different, meaning for each.
- Write a scene with two characters in an active car accident. One character is flying out the window while the other character is crushed under the steering wheel. They are experiencing the accident at the same time (in stage time) but in vastly different ways and, possibly, at different speeds.
- Close your eyes. Visualize your dream coming true. Open your eyes. Write that monologue or scene, that moment of your best wish coming true. How does that moment feel? What senses do you use to describe it? Life is hard. Enjoy the pleasure of getting lost in your dream.

Overview

Sometimes, we write for enjoyment or to strengthen our practice. This is especially important when you are in between writing plays. Writing prompts keep your skills sharp.

Writing Prompt: Silence

This writing prompt about how to use silence effectively onstage is an adaptation of a prompt shared by playwright Stef Smith of *Nora: A Doll's House.*[2] This is a longer, more involved prompt that will take about an hour.

- For ten minutes, make a list of memorable moments in your life that have happened in silence. These moments can be long or short; they can be real, from dreams, or even imagined. Think about why this moment was so impactful for you. (i.e., When my first girlfriend walked away after breaking up with me, and I felt abandoned by her when she was all I had in the world. I was afraid I'd be alone forever.)
- Select one of those moments.
- For 15 minutes, write a monologue* where Friend A is telling Friend B about that moment.
- For 15 minutes, turn the monologue into a dialogue* where Friend A is telling Friend B about the moment, but Friend B doesn't believe the moment ever happened.
- Now, edit the dialogue down to 20 lines, ten lines said by each character. You may add stage

directions,* but they should be minimal (a max of four directions of one line each). These 20 lines will be the core lines of your text for the next parts of the exercise; you will use those lines as the jumping-off point for the next step of the exercise multiple times.

- Then, copy and paste the 20 lines of dialogue. Next, remove three lines of dialogue and/or stage directions and replace them with silence.
- Then, copy and paste the 20 lines of dialogue. Next, remove six lines of dialogue and/or stage directions and replace them with silence.
- Then, copy and paste the 20 lines of dialogue. Next, remove ten lines of dialogue and/or stage directions and replace them with silence.
- You now have four versions of the same scene. Reflect on them. How has silence added to or subtracted from the dramatic tension in the scene? What exposition* did you think you needed but really didn't? Where did you use subtext? How did this increase or decrease the conflict in the scene?

Overview

Playwrights use exercises like this one to ensure they are creating a piece that will live meaningfully in breath, in time, in space on the stage; this both makes the play more engaging and helps reduce the overwriting that makes some plays feel like a piece of literary fiction.

Bracket Your Practice

Some playwrights find it useful to [bracket] their writing practice. This means they have a tradition of beginning and/or ending their practice the same way. I know writers who do yoga, listen to music, or find another way to separate their writing time from the rest of their life. This lends a sacredness to the moment. It also trains your brain – when you do [this thing] then your brain needs to shift into writing mode.

Of course, having the time alone to [bracket your practice] is a privilege. There are many mornings that I finish a scene over cold cereal with the kids screaming in the background. But if you [bracket] with general consistency, it can help make your writing a less stressful, more joyful experience.

Overview

Find ways to enrich your creative practices that fit the needs of your daily life.

Fun Fact

Fourth Wall: This is a theatrical convention where the performers on stage pretend not to see the audience and the theatrical event continues as if the audience is not there. This idea is often attributed to playwright Denis Diderot of *The Illegitimate Son*, who wrote in 1758 that actors and writers should "imagine a huge wall across the front of the stage, separating you from the audience, and behave exactly as if the curtain had never risen."[3]

Resources

Additional Resource

- *The Playwright's Toolbox: Exercises from 56 Contemporary Dramatists on Designing, Building, and Refurbishing Your Plays* by Justin Maxwell. Focus on Chapter 2, *Prewriting.* (Applause, 2024)

Discussed in Chapter

- *The Illegitimate Son* by Denis Diderot translated by Kiki Gounaridou and John Hellweg (Peter Lang Inc., 2011)
- *Nora: A Doll's House* by Stef Smith (Nick Hern Books)
- *Topdog/Underdog* by Suzan-Lori Parks (Theatre Communications Group)

Notes

1 Suzan Lori-Parks, Goodreads Quotes, https://www.good reads.com/quotes/tag/playwright
2 Printed with permission of playwright, 2024.
3 Cuddon, J. A. (2012). *Dictionary of Literary Terms and Literary Theory.* John Wiley & Sons.

1
Now and You

Theatre is about the Now. If a play lives for centuries to come, that's great. But we write for living audiences, living artists, and life itself. Playwriting is also about You, your perspective, and your lens on the world today. Embrace the now and have confidence in your voice.

"Becoming" as an Artist

You and I, we are always Becoming. We are becoming the artists we will be tomorrow, next year, and a decade from now. The perspective of your plays will reflect that becoming, and that's good; that helps make your plays interesting, alive, and complex – just like you are.

Part of Becoming is trying new things, finding success, making mistakes, recognizing those mistakes, and tackling an exercise again. Jumping off artistic cliffs with wild abandon. Going splat against the rocks a few times (or a few hundred times). Whatever happens artistically in your process is good as long as you learn and grow from it.

 DOI: 10.4324/9781003505310-3

Overview

Don't be afraid to fail. Sometimes, we learn more from our failures than our successes. Embrace the evolution of yourself and your artistry.

Being in Relationship

The theatrical experience is about the artist being in conversation with the world today, often asking questions about it, having an opinion about it, or wanting to share their point of view of it. Into this conversation, the artist invites another person – the audience – and the audience accepts the invitation.

In live performance, the artist and the audience explicitly agree to breathe together; to share this time, space, and experience. This live connection – this moment in time they share – creates a unique bond between the artist and audience, amplifying the impact of the shared experience in a way that changes them both.

In fact, the word "theatre" is rooted in the Greek "theatron" which means a place of seeing. It's a place of literal seeing – where the audience sits to see the performer – but also a metaphorical seeing of the world in a new way, through someone else's eyes, as they experience the same moment. This "seeing" can take place anywhere at any time; on a traditional proscenium stage, a backyard, in a basement, or in a classroom. Theatre thrives on the relationship between the artist and the audience in a live context, and that can happen anywhere – even online.

We sometimes write text for the stage by ourselves in a private room, but it's not fully theatre until it is shared with others. This is one reason that I enjoy playwriting: I never end up alone.

In *The Empty Space,* director Peter Brook says: "I can take any empty space and call it a bare stage. A man walks across this empty space whilst someone else is watching him, and this is all that is needed for an act theatre to be engaged."[1]

Throughout this process, I encourage you to write what you are passionate about with no limitations. I also encourage you to embrace the sacred relationship between artist and audience, which is the core of the theatrical experience. It is this relationship that will shape your play as it moves from the writing and revision process to the stage. However, this relationship should not stop you from writing or allow the fear of "what people will think" to override your creative process.

Playwright Jeremy O. Harris of *Slave Play* says:

> You constantly have some imposter syndrome. You think, "I'm not supposed to be here! Any move I make will reveal the mistake of this entire enterprise!" That's the main thing that I try and stamp out as a writer because what I like about myself is that most of the plays I have written, I wasn't writing thinking that I was a genius or that anyone

else would say I was a genius. I was writing because that was what I wanted to see. I wrote down what I wanted to see unabashedly, and I didn't worry about whether an audience would be shocked by this thing or that. If I don't want to see the play I'm writing, there's literally no reason for it to exist, which is one of the hard things about being a writer.[2]

The liveness of theatre begins with a person responding to the world at this very moment in time. So, write what you dare not say in your everyday life. Write what you do say awkwardly in the everyday, but make it louder, faster, funnier, and more daring for the stage. Make big choices and write with abandon.

Overview

We write and create for audiences today, and because we create for audiences today, that impacts how we think about our work.

We are here because . . .

The first day of class, I ask my students to think about why they are here, right now, in this moment, in this room, with these people, for this amount of time. This helps us connect with the immediacy of this moment and this process. Then we write a few *I am here because . . .* statements.

I'll share some of my "because" statements with you, and then I hope you will write your own.

I am here because . . .

Because writing is the way I understand the world.

Because writing is the way I understand myself.

Because it can be beauty.

Because it means I can get a babysitter and leave the kids behind.

Because it makes me feel better and improves my mood.

Because it is an important practice to me even when it's hard.

Because it can be the destruction you live through and come out whole.

You are here because . . .

I am here because _____.

I am here because _____.

I am here because _____.

I am here because _____.

I am here because _____.

I am here because _____.

I am here because _____.

Overview

Feel free to continue listing your "because" statements as you move through the experience of this book. They can be a powerful reminder of why we are here. Some playwrights post their "because" statements (and other statements of meaning) close to their writing space so they can draw power from them at any time.

Resources
Student Favorites

The plays listed here were some of my students' favorites over the years for illustrating the different ways plays can be in conversation with the world:

- *The Cherry Orchard* by Anton Chekov (Methuen)
  - Set in pre-revolutionary Russia, it tells the story of a family struggling with the impending loss of their beloved home.

- *Let Me Down Easy* by Anna Deavere Smith (Theatre Communications Group)
  - This drama is taken from direct contemporary interviews by the performer-playwright exploring issues surrounding healthcare in the U.S.A.

- *School Girls; Or, The African Mean Girls Play* by Jocelyn Bioh (Methuen)
  - Queen Bee Paulina awaits the arrival of the Miss Ghana pageant recruiter. A comedy about friendship, community, and moral and ethical decision-making.

- *Yellowface* by David Henry Hwang (Theatre Communications Group)
  - An exploration of Asian identity and the ever-changing definition of what it is to be an American and embrace the American Dream.

- *By the Bog of Cats* by Marina Carr (Faber)

- Loosely based on Euripides' tragedy *Medea*, this is the prophetic tale of Hester Swane, an Irish Traveler, who attempts to come to terms with a lifetime of abandonment.

Additional Resource

- *Performance Studies: The Basics* by Andreea S. Micu is a good read for those interested in the academic discipline of Performance Studies, which uses live performance as a lens and tool to study the world. (Routledge, 2021)

Discussed in Chapter

- *The Empty Space* by Peter Brook (Penguin Classics)
- *Slave Play* by Jeremy O. Harris (New York Theatre Workshop Bookshop)

Notes

1 *The Empty Space* by Peter Brook, Penguin Classics; 47456th edition, 1994.
2 *The Creative Independent* interview with Jeremy O. Harris "On Believing in Yourself" by Lior Phillips, https://thecreativeindependent.com/people/playwright-jeremy-o-harris-on-shifting-the-shape-of-theater/, 2022.

2
Character

We begin with creating characters because – regardless of structure, form, or genre – at least one character will be the heart and soul of your play. We watch theatre to engage with characters who are having an experience that holds meaning for them and the audience.

What are Characters?

Characters* are the raw materials for your new play.

They can be human. They can also be objects, animals, nature, imaginary creatures, or anything else you want them to be. There is no limit.

Regardless of the form that your characters take, it is their wants and desires that are the dramatic engine of your play; these wants and desires can move your characters forwards or backwards or even cause them to stand still. But they still want something, even if that desire is – as Brook puts it – to simply walk across a room.

Before we can dive into uncovering a character's wants and desires, we need to know a bit about them.

DOI: 10.4324/9781003505310-4

21

Writing Exercise

Begin creating a character by answering the questions below. If you get stuck, grab a magazine or newspaper, rip out a picture that includes at least one person, and answer the following questions. There is no right or wrong answer; just write.

You can create as many characters as you wish. But I suggest that you create at least three to generate ample material for future exercises.

NOTE: If you are working from a character who already exists in a short play or other material you are writing, start answering these questions fresh. If your character evolves as you learn more about them, follow their lead.

- Name(s):
- City of Residence:
- Occupation:
- Age:
- Partner:
- Kids:
- City of residence:
- Description of home:
- Passion(s):
- Biggest fear:
- If there was no law to stop them, how far would they go to avoid facing their biggest fear:
- What is the biggest lie they have told and why:
- What would they do if the lie was uncovered and there was no rule of law to shape their actions:
- Most embarrassing moment:
- Favorite movie and why:

- Favorite book and why:
- What object(s) do they display in their bedroom (their private space, the place that is most intimate to them):
- What object(s) do they display in their living room (their public space, the place where they will be judged by others):
- If their home was on fire and they could grab one object to save, what would they grab and why:
- Have they ever been violent? If so, under what circumstances:
- What would they want to yell at someone:
- If they could snap their fingers and one person would disappear from their lives, who would this person be:
- Why do they want that person to disappear and how far would they go to make this happen:
- How would your character's obituary read:
- How would your character want their obituary to read:

Now, reflect on: What did you learn from exploring your character? What did you already know? What surprised you?

You can use this exercise as a springboard to create new characters or to learn more about a character you've already created.

In pre-writing exercises like this one, the goal is to get to know your character(s) intimately. You may or may not use these specifics in your final play, but you are more likely to write compelling, engaging characters because you know them so well.

We see an example of using a specific detail of a character's life to shape the play in *Anna in the Tropics* by playwright Nilo Cruz. Cruz creates Juan, a man who is hired as a lector to read to the workers in a cigar factory. Juan reads *Anna Karenina* to the workers and each has a different reaction to the book. The workers' reactions spark conflicts in their relationships. These conflicts are the dramatic engine that moves the play forward. Cruz uses a specific book that Juan favors to inform his storytelling in a powerful way.

There are many ways to generate characters. As you learn more about your creative process, you'll discover ways to create characters that work for you.

> I use a lot of acting exercises. The whole thing of really imagining the backstory of your character . . . . Even if you don't need it for the play, you as a writer know your character and then I think little bits of detail will come out through the play that you are unaware of and that flesh out the character.
>
> Playwright In-Sook Chappell of *P'yongyang*[1]

Writing Exercise

Like actors, playwrights examine the everyday activities of their characters to learn more about them.

Select one of the characters that you generated from the previous exercise.

(1) Write a short paragraph about what the character likes to do on their day off.

(2) Now, let's dive more deeply into the details of their day:

- What time would they get up on their day off? Why?
- What's their favorite breakfast on a day off? Perhaps go and have breakfast in a location that they would enjoy. Now, go and have breakfast in a location that they would dislike. What is the difference between these two spaces? What would make them love/dislike them? What does that tell you about the preferences and temperament of your character?
- What would they wear on their day off? (Write a short description, sketch it, or do a bit of online clothes browsing.)
- What would ruin that day for them?
- What would they love to happen on that day?
- Now, where would they shop for groceries on their day off? Either go to or browse online that supermarket. Make lists of what they would put in their cart. How much would this all cost? Can they afford all of this – do they go name brand or generic to save money? What does what this character chooses to buy tell you? For example, it can tell you small things (they hate vegetables!) or big things (they spend way more on wine than they can afford).
- Feel free to continue to flesh out the details of their day-off to inform your writing. Remember, we're not worried about finding the "right" answer. Instead, we're curiously exploring our character without judgement.

(3) Now, pick any other answer(s) to your character questions in the earlier exercise and take 15 minutes to digger deeper into why this detail is important to your character.

For example, if you select "If their home was on fire and they could grab one object to save, what would they grab and why?" then you could describe the object: how does it feel or taste? What was the moment the character received the object? How did that moment feel? Was there a sound or touch experience associated with that moment?

Details like these give you a sensory experience of your character, which adds to your understanding of them.

Overview

Characters are the core of your play. They can be anything you want them to be, but it is their wants and desires that will shape your piece. It's useful to begin exploring their lives to understand their personalities, preferences, wants, desires, and more.

The Specific Becomes the Universal

Playwright A.B. Yehoshua of *Mr. Mani* says, "Art has the ability to transcend language and culture, it speaks to the universal human experience."[2]

Throughout the writing process, you'll learn about your characters, and that knowledge will influence your writing. Learn as much as possible about your characters. The more specific your characters are, the more universal their stories become, even if that feels counterintuitive at first.

By writing your character's experiences with specificity, audiences connect more deeply with the underlying concerns of the universal human condition.

For example, we see this occur in playwright Ludvig Holberg's *Jeppe on the Hill* (18th century). In this excerpt, Nille, the wife of Jeppe, is addressing the audience at the beginning of the play because she is frustrated with Jeppe's behavior:

NILLE

> I don't believe there is such a lazy rascal in the
> whole district as my husband. I can hardly
> wake him up when I pull him out of bed by the
> hair. Today the rascal knows that it is market
> day, but still he lies and sleeps so long. [The
> Preacher] said to me lately, "Nille, you are too
> hard on your husband. He is and ought to be
> master of the household." But I answered him,
> "No, my dear [Preacher], if I should let him
> boss this house for a single year then neither
> the landlord would get his rent nor the [Church
> their] fee, since he would squander in drink all
> that I have in the house. Should I let such a man
> rule this household, who is ready to sell farm,
> wife, children – yes, even himself – for drink?"
> Whereupon [the Preacher] became silent and
> thoughtfully stroked his chin.

The overseer of the estate sides with me and says, "Little woman, don't you mind what the Preacher says. Although the ritual says that you must honor and obey your husband, your lease, which is newer than the ritual, says that you must keep up your place and pay your rent, which it would be impossible for you to do if you did not drag your old man out of bed by the hair every morning and drive him to work."

Just now I jerked him out of bed . . . . Hey, Jeppe, aren't you up yet, you lazy bones? Hey, Jeppe, come out!

In this excerpt, Nille describes very specific problems she's having with her husband and a specific conversation with the Preacher. Even though the play was written over 300 years ago, by using specific details of her issues with her husband, we understand her aggravation and connect with her plight. Who hasn't had a partner or family member who drives them crazy by their laziness or annoying behavior? Nille's complaints about her husband resonate with us even today because they are specific, and with specificity comes universality.

Writing with specificity also applies to selecting specific details to showcase in your play – like a piece of music or a piece of furniture – that connect the characters. The specificity of that detail tells us more about the entire situation.

For example, in playwright Yasmina Reza's *Art*, a specific painting is key to understanding both the story and the themes* of the play.

In *Art,* the relationship between three lifelong friends (Marc, Serge, and Yvan) is fractured when Serge buys a painting that is entirely white for a large amount of money. Is this Art? Is it an enormous waste of money? What does this say about Serge, that he would spend so much money on a painting that is, essentially, a blank canvas? What does it say about Marc and Yvan that they are friends with Serge?

While the conflict between friends begins with the painting, it escalates to become about more difficult (and previously hidden) aspects of their friendship including trust, betrayal, and control.

By the end of the play, the three men gradually put their friendship back together, but they are changed due to this disagreement over Art, which – in the end – was both about a specific piece of art and, more powerfully, the art of friendship over a lifetime.

All of us have had a friendship that changes over time. So, the specificity of the friendships in *Art* leads to a universality within the story that we can grasp. We connect with the underlying universality of how friendships change, even if we don't know anything about painting.

Even plays that are set in the more metaphorical genres of fairytales and fables have specific characters and worlds.

For example, playwright David Harrower's *Knives in Hens* is a fable set in a pre-industrial landscape and features a character known only as Young Woman. However, at the beginning of the play, the playwright immediately begins defining who she is as a character and the world in which she lives very specifically; he shares with us the exterior landscape and inner life of each character. Within the first three pages, we learn:

- They live in a cottage at the end of a village in a rural place;
- They work on a farm;
- The farm requires hard labor with no modern equipment;
- The Young Woman is very curious and asks questions that are practical, spiritual, and theoretical;
- Her Husband does not care for her questions and thinks he's smarter than she is, even though we can see he is not;
- The Young Woman lives in her head and in the realm of ideas;
- The Husband lives in the real world, interacting only with whatever is in front of him;
- There is a negative tension in the marriage.

Immediately, the playwright focuses on the visceral specificity of these characters. Through that specificity, we begin to connect with the characters, even though we don't know what the story is about yet.

Writing Prompt: The Five "Whys"

To understand the deeper truth as to "Why" your character is doing something, pick one important moment in their lives.

Now, ask "Why" this character behaved this way in that specific moment. Jot down an explanation quickly on a list; don't overthink it.

Now, ask "Why" four more times. Each time, go deeper within your character's psyche.

For example, a character overreacts and shoots his neighbor. **Why?** Because he was angry at the neighbor for feeding his dog bad food and making it sick. **Why?** Because he loves that dog like a family member, he had a terrible day at work, and he has a violent temper. **Why?** Because the dog is the only family he has left. His human family refuses to speak to him due to his violent temper which has negatively impacted their lives. **Why?** Because his terrible temper is the way he tries to control those around him. If he forces them to do what he wishes, he feels more in control in the world. **Why?** Deep down he hates feeling out of control and impotent in a world that is uncontrollable by humans. His terrible temper is really just a symptom of his anger at being impotent in the world.

Now, we know one powerful element of his personality is his violent temper. We can decide how to use his violent temper when he comes into conflict with other characters. Or, we can decide that we don't want our character to have a violent temper and so we re-envision the character (removing this element of his personality).

After you make five lists, ask yourself: What have you learned that you did not know before? What connections have been made clear? Are any of these connections surprising to you? If so, how are they surprising, and do they change the course of the character's journey?

As you write, ask yourself "Why" a character is doing something, and ask that question many times. These reasons you discover will inform your writing.

Overview

The more specific your characters are, the more universal their stories become.

Don't Censor Your Characters

Just like actual people, characters can be "good," "bad," and everything in between. They harbor the promise of perfection and the heartbreak of failure. While you're learning about them, don't judge them. Just let them evolve, change, and speak their minds. By fearlessly exploring your characters, you will create lives with complexity, dynamism, and depth.

Playwright Eisa Davis of *Angela's Mixtape* wrote the poem *If You Do Not Lie* about being open and honest with yourself when writing. Here is a short excerpt:

> when you don't lie,
> when you adhere to your deepest fantasies,
> memories, nightmares, obsessions,
> loves and hatreds

like a molecule holds its atoms,
when these obsessions are your very best friends,
when you are set upon by them,
possessed by them,
when they *must out*, you don't sleep.
and when you are awake,
you are not in service to anything but them.[3]

I find Davis's exhortation empowering: to live your art through the truths that burn within you. I encourage you to embrace "your deepest fantasies, memories, nightmares, obsessions, loves and hatreds" as you write. These passions set your play on fire.

Remember, pre-writing is just for you so your characters can be who they really are in front of you. You may never show your pre-writing to anyone, but it will shape how you write their stories.

Writing Exercise

Now that you know a bit about your characters' external everyday reality, let's explore what fills their fantasy life. Write narratives, make lists, draw pictures, or otherwise illustrate the answers to the following questions. Be as specific as possible. Each question can have multiple answers.

- What real-life fantasy/daydream(s) do they have that could come true? (e.g., standing up to their boss)

- What unreal fantasy/daydream(s) do they have? (e.g., the ability to fly)
- What reoccurring nightmare(s) do they have? (e.g., being drowned in a lake)
- What reoccurring good dream(s) do they have? (e.g., hugging a friend who is far away)
- Now, look at the material you've generated overall. What have you learned about what they hope for? What have you learned about what they are afraid of?

Our fantasies are entwined with our most powerful hopes and fears. Exploring the hopes and fears of your characters can help you rapidly deepen your understanding of them. Playwrights revisit these types of pre-writing activities as they write their plays to stay in touch with the character's inner life.

Overview

The more honest you can be about your characters in the pre-writing stage, the more you can write about them with specificity and grace later on. You are looking for their sacred Truths. And our Truths are often as messy and complex as we are.

Protagonist/Antagonist/Conflict

Characters feel something deeply and are compelled to act on it – whether it's a commitment to changing the world or a commitment to ignoring it, a commitment to make something happen, or a commitment to prevent something from happening. The Protagonist(s) and Antagonist(s) have opposing desires that are in Conflict and cannot exist at the same time.

Sometimes, you will know what a character wants at the beginning of your writing process. Sometimes, you learn what they want through pre-writing or by living their lives through multiple drafts.

Here are the definitions:

- **Protagonist***: A character going after something, a goal*, usually the main focus of the play.
- **Antagonist***: A character who opposes the protagonist's goals, usually the secondary focus of the play.
- **Conflict***: A struggle between opposing forces in a play, often characters who are in opposition to one another because they want different things. The conflict may occur within a character as well as between characters. If the conflict occurs within a character, then the playwright finds a way to externalize that conflict onstage.

Sometimes, there is a misconception that the protagonist is the "good guy," the antagonist is the "bad guy," and the conflict is about good triumphing over evil. While that can be the play you choose to write, it does not have to be. For example, the protagonists and antagonists might be friends who disagree – like *Art* – or a husband and wife whose love has grown cold – like *Knives in Hens.* Choosing the protagonist, antagonist, and conflict are just a few of the artistic decisions you'll make in your writing process.

Overview

A protagonist is a character going after something, and an antagonist is a character in opposition to the protagonist's goal. Conflict is created by their opposition.

Why is Having a "Want" Important?

A character wanting something gives us a reason to watch. We spend our time at the theater to see something happen within and/or between characters.

The character's "want" is a part of their goal. The protagonist wants to achieve the goal. The antagonists "want" to stop them from achieving their goal.

The characters' "wants" are rooted in an emotional truth that's larger and more important than the actual want itself. The "want" is a vehicle for a larger truth.

For example, let's say a character wants their father to attend their graduation ceremony. The father is not sure he wants to come. Throughout the play, the character will try different ways to reach their goal – to persuade the father to attend – because the character wants him at the ceremony.

Through this journey, we learn that the child and father have been estranged for many years – the character's strong want to have their father at the ceremony is not just about the ceremony. The character's want is driven by their underlying need to receive unconditional love from their father. The character's want is just a vehicle for the larger truth of desiring deep, abiding, unconditional love from a parent.

This is an example of how specificity, asking "why," and locating a "want" work together to help a playwright create a play.

There are many ways that "wants" can inform a play. Regardless of how you use a "want" in your play, it is the dramatic engine that drives your play forward and makes audiences lean in to learn how the play turns out.

Here are examples of different ways to use "wants" from the plays *House of Desires, The Miser,* and *Katie Roche.*

(1) *House of Desires* by Juana Inés de la Cruz

A very clear example of how different characters' "wants" come into direct conflict is in *House of Desires.*

In *Desires,* Lenor and Carlos are in love. Lenor's father, Don Rodrigo, disapproves of her marrying Carlos, so Lenor and Carlos make plans to run away together. There are very clear wants for all characters involved:

- Lenor and Carlo are in love and want to stay together no matter how Don Rodrigo feels.
- Don Rodrigo disapproves of the marriage, so he wants to stop it at all costs.

Lenor, Carlo, and Don Rodrigo go after their wants. This leads to a humorous love story full of mistaken identities, daring deeds, and comic confusions. At the end of the play, Lenor and Carlo get what they wanted in the beginning – they remain together, happily in love. Their want is fulfilled, and Don Rodrigo's want is not.

By having the lover's want fulfilled, the play's theme emerges, which is that true love will overcome all obstacles* in its way. (Later in the book, we'll discuss how a character's "want," and whether or not that "want" is fulfilled, shows the audience the themes of the play.)

(2) *The Miser* by Moliére

Here's an example of another way a playwright uses a character's "want" in a play: A character might openly express one want but secretly want something else. By expressing one thing – but showing that they secretly want something else – the tension between what the character says and what they do makes us sit forward, interested in what's going to happen next.

In *The Miser,* Valère falls in love with Élise, so he gets a job as a servant in her home. This allows Valère to get close to Élise and win her love.

- Valére's spoken want – to get the job – is really a cover for his real want – to win Élise's heart.
- Élise's father becomes convinced that Valère does not want the job but wants to steal his and Élise's money.
- Valére's secret want unintentionally puts him into conflict with Élise's father – which further complicates his attempts to get Élise to love and marry him.

The conflict engages us and makes us wonder what will happen next; the conflict gives us a reason to continue watching the play.

In addition, these conflicting wants in the play ask deeper questions about true love: how do you know when someone loves you versus when they just want you for your money?

(3) *Katie Roche* by Teresa Deevy

However, not all characters know exactly what they want or how to achieve it. It's the search for their want – and their success or failure in identifying and achieving it – that makes an interesting story.

In *Katie Roche,* the leading character, Katie Roche, has a life crisis; she is faced with an unhappy marriage and does not know how to create a happy life, especially given the strict gender and economic rules of 1930s Ireland.

We see that she is capable of autonomy and leading an independent life, but every time she has an opportunity to change her situation, some social stricture or her own doubts about her abilities keep her from acting on the possibility.

By the end of the play, she resigns herself to an unhappy marriage. While she doesn't necessarily want to be in an unhappy marriage, she does think that she can't make change, so her "want" becomes to try and make the best of a bad situation. Her specific journey illuminates the universal reality of how we – both individually and as a society – undermine our own happiness.

These are just three examples of how a character's want informs a play.

Regardless of how you fashion the "want," it is the dramatic engine of the play. It makes the audience interested to watch the play and see how it turns out.

Overview

There are many ways that a character might engage with their wants and desires. Their wants and desires might be large or small but are usually anchored in a deeper Truth. A character wanting something gives your play an engine that propels them and engages the audience throughout the play.

Key Moments

Key moments* are moments in your character's life that forever stay with your character and shape the way they think and behave. These key moments can be large or small moments in the world, but they all have a significant impact on your character.

For example, if a character had wonderful parents who gave them confidence, then when this character faced adversity, perhaps that confidence would give them the emotional strength to persevere.

Another example: if a character was harmed by an ex-boyfriend, then they might not want to date again and risk being hurt.

As you discover these key moments, keep a list of them. When you get stuck, you can return to those key moments and think about how the scene you are writing might be impacted by that experience.

Overview

Make sure to highlight any moments that seem important (or Key) to your character's history, belief systems, and actions. These Key Moments can help you unlock your play.

Resources
Student Favorites

The plays listed here were some of my students' favorites for illustrating the lessons in this chapter.

- *Back of the Throat* by Yussef El Guindi (Dramatists Play Service)
  - *Back of the Throat* is the story of an apparently friendly visit by two government officials, which soon devolves into a full-blown, no-holds-barred probe and examination of what it means to be an American.

- *Cambodian Rock Band* by Lauren Yee (Concord Theatricals) and Music by Dengue Fever (Original Cast Recording available on Apple Music)
  - *Cambodian Rock Band* is a riveting play with music. In 1978, Chum fled Cambodia and narrowly escaped the murderous Khmer Rouge

regime. Thirty years later, he returns in search of his wayward daughter, Neary. As the play jumps back and forth in time, thrilling mystery meets rock concert until both father and daughter are forced to face the music of the past.

- *Cost of Living* by Martyna Majok (Theatre Communications Group)
  - *Cost of Living* is the heartfelt exploration of two relationships: one between a wealthy graduate student with cerebral palsy and his female caregiver, the other between a woman recovering from a terrible accident being tended to by her ex-husband.

Additional Resource

- *The Subtext* podcast hosted by Brian James Polak features interviews by playwrights about their creative processes (available on major podcast outlets).

Discussed in Chapter

- *Angela's Mixtape* by Eisa Davis (53rd State Press)
- *Anna in the Tropics* by Nilo Cruz (Theatre Communications Group)
- *Art* by Yasmina Reza (Farrar, Straus and Giroux)
- *House of Desires* by Juana Inés de la Cruz (Oberon)
- *Jeppe on the Hill* by Ludvig Holberg (circa 1722/ translated from Danish by Waldemar C. Westergaard and Martin B. Rudd/Project Gutenberg/ eBook #42022)

- *Katie Roche* by Teresa Deevy (Mint Theater Books)
- *Knives in Hens* by David Harrower (Methuen)
- *Mr. Mani* by A.B. Yehoshua (Contemporary Drama from Israel/Loki Books)
- *The Miser* by Molière (Project Gutenberg/eBook 6923)
- *P'yongyang* by In-Sook Chappell (Oberon)

Notes

1 *Playwrights Series: Character*, National Theatre, posted on YouTube on January 26, 2018.
2 BookKey,https://www.bookey.app/quote-author/ab-yehoshua#art-has-the--27
3 *If You Do Not Lie* by Eisa Davis, from "Adrienne Kennedy: A Liberating Beacon," Originally appeared in *American Theatre* magazine, September 2019. Read the entire poem here:americantheatre.org/2019/09/04/adrienne-kennedy-a-liberating-beacon/

3

Externalization

Audiences engage with our show physically through their five sense – sight, smell, hearing, taste, and touch. Very few will ever read our words on the page. So, it's important to learn how to write plays that externalize the internal workings of our characters.

Externalizing Wants and Desires

What is happening within your characters – their wants and desires – must be externalized so that we can see them onstage. This is one reason long-running television shows like *Law & Order* are so popular – the characters either desperately want, or do not want, the crime to be solved, and it is easy to externalize those conflicts.

There are many ways to externalize internal conflicts.

For example, characters can speak their conflicts into the world, agreeing and disagreeing with one another, making plans and trying to execute them while thwarting the plans of others. Playwrights activate conversations by layering different wants, desires, fears, and needs underneath the language – giving the language a dramatic propulsion all its own that's as powerful as a punch or kick.

   DOI: 10.4324/9781003505310-5

For example, in playwright Athol Fugard's *"Master Harold" . . . and the boys,* Sam remains a servant at home while Hally goes off to school and gains power and prestige. In their society, Hally ascends to the higher social status of "Master" while Sam remains a servant at home.

Throughout the play, Sam calls Hally by his nickname ("Hally") because they are close friends. However, at the end of the play, Sam changes and calls Hally the formal "Master Harold" because he feels Hally has betrayed and deserted him so they are no longer friends. Sam changing Hally's name – from a nickname that a friend uses to a formal name that non-friends use – is an externalization of the broken relationship between the men.

Here are a few more examples of different ways to externalize your characters inner lives:

- In playwright Edward Albee's *Three Tall Women,* he externalizes the conflict within his mother by creating characters that represent his Mother at different ages.
  - The three characters are named A, B, and C.
  - They are fully embodied characters with their own wants, needs, and desires, and their own point of views.
  - Splitting his mother's internal life into three different characters allows Albee to tease apart the complex emotional journey of her life in a way that the audience can perceive; the characters interact and show us what the Mother is otherwise feeling inside.

- In playwright Victoria Nalani Kneubuhl's play *The Bones Live,* she externalizes conflicts and inner lives by setting the play both today and in the 19th century. In the story, academic and cultural consultant Kawehi travels home to Hawai'i after a work trip in Berlin, but she's got a secret in her bag: a set of Hawai'ian bones she discovered in a German museum.

  - Kneubuhl sets scenes both in present day with Kawehi and in the 19th Century when the bones were handled by western European academics who did not understand Hawai'ian traditions.

  - By having scenes set both in present day and in the past, we can literally see the differences between the past and present, and experience the ripple effects of history – how the assumptions of the past lead to conflict in the present.

  - The characters in both time periods go on a journey to navigate cultural shifts and to better understand themselves.

- In playwright Jean Genet's *The Maids,* he externalizes the conflict by having two characters act out their wants and desires.

  - Solange and Claire are two sisters who work as maids for a wealthy family. While their boss (the Madame) is away, they take turns role-playing Madame.

  - By taking turns playing different roles (one playing a maid and another playing Madame), the audience can see the abuse that Maids suffer under Madame's rule. Through the role play, we see how social norms and expectations allow the abuse to continue.

- At the end of the play, the final scene suggests the Maids have made the decision to murder Madame when she gets home.

The externalizations of your characters wants and desires are influenced by external factors including:

- the time period of the story
- the geographic location of the story
- the style of the storytelling (e.g., realism*, horror, absurdist)

As playwrights, the obvious external factors also help shape the character's externalized wants and desires so the audience understands the play.

For example, in Fugard's *"Master Harold" . . . and the boys* discussed previously, the setting is 1950. So, the characters adhere to social conventions of the 1950s. This helps us understand the characters' conflicts because those conflicts are rooted in the history of the time period. The external circumstances help shape externalization of the character's journey.

Writing Exercise

One way to explore what a character wants is to put the character in different situations, talking to different people, so they can express their wants in new ways.

Select a character you've created:

- What would they tell their boss in a board room that they want professionally?

- What would they tell their lover in a bedroom that they want out of their relationship?
- What would they promise their dying parent in the hospital that the character will do after the parent is gone?
- What would they tell a good friend they want out of life in a private moment in their living room?
- What would they tell a new acquaintance what they want out of life on a public bus?

Reflect on your answers. Where are there intersections or resonances between wants? (i.e., Do their professional goals overlap with their promise to their dying parent?) What wants feel the most compelling and powerful to you. What goals are you excited to write about?

Take time to elaborate on any want(s) that excite you. Keep that material nearby to use in future exercises.

There is no one right or wrong way to discover your characters wants and desires, the important thing is that you discover them and then figure out how to externalize them.

Overview

Externalizing wants and desires is important to do onstage because the audience is experiencing the characters in the moment. In a book, the readers can re-read a scene or read thoughts unexpressed physically but, in theatre, on the stage, audiences cannot read your play. So, you must write the play for it to be perceived onstage.

What About Likeability?

Your characters do not need to be likable but they do need to be compelling. Many theatre pieces have main characters who do bad things, but we still love to watch them onstage. For example, Shakespeare's Lear in *King Lear*, Sondheim's Mrs. Lovett in *Sweeney Todd*, and Schaffer's Saleri in *Amadeus*:

- Lear is a King who terrorizes his daughters to try to control his legacy and his kingdom long after he is gone.
- Mrs. Lovett is a pie shop owner who mercilessly murders rich men both to make a living and to prove her devotion to Sweeney Todd so that he will love her.
- Saleri is a famous composer who ruthlessly tries to destroy Mozart – his competition – while pretending to be Mozart's friend so that he will become the most revered composer of all time.

You would not want to encounter these people in real life, but they make excellent theatre.

Characters need to be compelling.

Usually, what makes characters compelling is that they are driving themselves to fulfill a personal want, regardless of the cost. If you write any character well, you will reveal both the good and bad, the shades of grey, within each of us. We can connect to a character who is doing a terrible thing if we understand *why* they are doing it. This is where our "5 Whys" exercise from earlier comes in handy. Asking "why" multiple times helps us understand the root of a character's behavior so we can dramatize it.

For example, in playwright Sam Shepard's ensemble play *The Curse of the Starving Class,* a family struggles to survive as working poor in the U.S.A. Characters scream at each other, piss on the floor, and physically abuse one another. Those same characters also comfort one another, love one another, and hold each other through long nights. No one in this play is particularly "likable," but neither are they "unlikable." We are compelled by them because we see the hardship they are facing – including hunger, pain, and the death of their dreams. Then we see their attempts to create a better life.

Audiences lean in because they are compelling characters, not "good" ones.

Overview

Your characters do not need to be likable but they do need to be compelling. They often become compelling by taking action to try and get what they want. Digging down into that "want," understanding what truth/emotion/ reality lies beneath, makes characters more compelling to watch.

Inspiration Is Everywhere

By this point in the book, some writers are struggling because they are more excited by a theme, location, image, or idea than by a character.

If that's you, simply ask yourself questions about who would be involved with that idea or live in that place. Here are a few questions to begin with:

- Let's say, I want to write about climate change. Then I'd ask myself, where is a place people would meet to talk about climate change? How would those people agree? How would those people disagree? What would a tree think about what they were saying? What would an ant think?
- Let's say, I really love this photograph of an empty restaurant. Then I'd ask myself, who would eat live in this setting? Why would they love it? Who would not eat live in this setting? Why would they hate it?
- Let's say, I think that painting is ugly. Then I'd ask myself, who would own this piece of art? What would it mean to them?

You can use what inspires you as a jumping-off point for creating compelling characters.

For example, playwright Harold Pinter of *The Caretaker* did not dig deeply into his characters' backstories at first. He heard a few lines of dialogue and then wrote forward, learning about the characters along the way.[1] However, once he learned about his characters, he revised with that knowledge in mind.[2]

However, as a beginning playwright, it is good to practice creating specific characters in detail. Later, you may choose to use this tool of character creation or not, but you will have it in your creative toolbox.

In addition, inspiration does not have to be tied so literally to your playwriting. I find that engaging with different forms of art, and even writing in different modes (for me, it's poetry), adds to my understanding of the world in all its complexity. Simply by feeding myself intellectually, spiritually, emotionally, and mentally by engaging more deeply with the world – looking beyond my front door – my writing shifts and evolves in new and exciting ways.

Thoughts on inspiration from playwright Ken Urban of A Guide for the Homesick, *whose music-making with his band Occurrence influences his playwriting*

I tend to hear my plays before I see them. I think my scripts like scores, and so I often listen to a reading or a rehearsal of my plays with my eyes closed, so I can really hear it.

Rhythm and tempo tell so much story, express so much about the inner life of a character in my work. No doubt, that is an influence of my work in the band as the lead song writer and producer. Oddly, in the band, I am not the prime lyricist. In fact, I prefer for Cat or Johnny (the two vocalists) to write lyrics, as I prefer to focus on the music and the overall sound and production. Music is a bit of a break from focusing on words. Sounds can be my words.

Overview

Inspiration for a play can come from any source. The work is to theatricalize that inspiration.

Resources
Student Favorites

The plays listed here were some of my students' favorites for illustrating the lessons in this chapter.

- *Bengal Tiger at the Baghdad Zoo* by Rajiv Joseph (Soft Skull)
  - A darkly comedic drama that looks on as the lives of two U.S. soldiers, an Iraqi translator, and a tiger intersect on the streets of Baghdad.
- *The Ferryman* by Jez Butterworth (Theatre Communications Group)
  - The Carney farmhouse in Northern Ireland is a hive of activity with preparations for the annual harvest until they are interrupted by a mysterious visitor.

Additional Resource

- Playwrights on narrative: youtu.be/QHS3tQDpTao?si=1KyO3G5aGO8LSV2z (National Theatre/London)

Discussed in Chapter

- *A Guide for the Homesick* by Ken Urban (Dramatists Play Service)
- *Amadeus* by Peter Shaffer (Harper)
- *The Bones Live* by Victoria Nalani Kneubuhl (*Island Plays*, University of Hawai'i Press)
- *The Caretaker* by Harold Pinter (*Complete Works, Volume 2*/Grove Press)
- *The Curse of the Starving Class* by Sam Shepard (*Seven Plays*/Dial Press)
- *King Lear* by William Shakespeare (Folger Library/Online)
- *The Maids* by Jean Genet (Grove Press)
- *"Master Harold" . . . and the Boys* by Athol Fugard (Vintage)
- *Occurrence* (band) with Ken Urban (occurrencemusic.com)
- *Sweeney Todd* by Stephen Sondheim and Hugh Wheeler (Musical/Applause)
- *Three Tall Women* by Edward Albee (Penguin)

Notes

1 Interview with Harold Pinter, *New York Times,* Arts & Leisure, 1979.
2 "Pinter's Revision of 'The Caretaker'," by G.M. Berkowitz, *Journal of Modern Literature*, 5(1), 1976, 109–116.

4
Monologue

A monologue is a story or speech given by a character in a play. They can also be very useful pre-writing activities when you are learning more about your character and their world.

Monologue

A monologue is a story or speech given by a character.

In pre-writing and early drafts, monologues are sometimes purely informational or explicitly provide backstory. These monologues are teaching the playwright more about their characters and their worlds.

However, monologues are the most engaging when the characters are actively working to towards a goal that will influence the character's journey and the arc of the play.

For example, in an active monologue, a character might try to persuade someone to do something.

In *The Glass Menagerie* by Tennessee Williams, Laura tries to convince her mother to stop forcing her to date. If Laura successfully convinces her mother to leave her alone, then Laura's quiet life continues as normal. If not, she loses her treasured life of quiet privacy. Here are a few lines of Laura's monologue:

> No, Mom, Please! I have to say this. I can't go outside these walls. There's just too much pain [in my damaged leg]! I can feel everyone staring at me-Staring at this. (*Laura points to her braced leg.*) The noise it makes, it's just so loud! It's why I dropped out of high school. I felt everyone's eyes staring at me, heard all the giggles they tried to suppress as I clomped and limped down the hall.[1]

Laura's passionate argument fails, and her mother forces her to date, which makes Laura's life more complicated, fueling future conflicts. This is an example of an active persuasive monologue, which has a powerful impact in the moment and also pushes the story forward.

Monologues can also be activated by helping a character make a decision.

For example, in *Dido, Queen of Carthage* by playwright Christopher Marlowe (16th-century), the Queen's monologue shows what she is thinking and feeling internally as well as helps her make an important decision that pushes the story forward. There are multiple steps to her process that build on one another within the monologue.

In the play, Dido is an independent queen who begins the play refusing to ever marry a man.

Then she is poisoned by Cupid, causing her to fall in love with Aeneas. When Aeneas decides to leave, she tries to stop him.

In this monologue, she begins by praising the natural forces (a storm) that brought Aeneas to her:

DIDO

O blessed tempests that did drive him in!
O happy sand that made him run aground!
Henceforth you shall be our Carthage gods.
Ay, but it may be, he will leave my love,
And seek a foreign land call'd Italy:
O that I had a charm to keep the winds
Within the closure of a golden ball;
Or that the Tyrrhene sea were in mine arms,
That he might suffer shipwreck on my breast,
As oft as he attempts to hoist up sail!

After wishing he would never leave, she decides that if natural forces do not keep him in Carthage, she will do all she can to prevent him from leaving. She instructs her servants to kidnap his son and sabotage his ships.

I must prevent him; wishing will not serve.
Go bid my nurse take young Ascanius,
And bear him in the country to her house;
Aeneas will not go without his son;
Yet, lest he should, for I am full of fear,
What if I sink his ships? O, he will frown!

As she's giving her servants these orders, she realizes that he will be unhappy staying in Carthage. But she decides it is better for him to stay and be unhappy than for her to kill herself out of grief that he has left her. Nothing scares her – not war or losing her empire or natural disaster – nothing terrifies her more than losing Aeneas.

> Better he frown than I should die of grief.
> I cannot see him frown; it may not be:
> Armies of foes resolv'd to win this town,
> Or impious traitors vow'd to have my life,
> Affright me not; only Aeneas' frown
> Is that which terrifies poor Dido's heart:
> Not bloody spears, appearing in the air,
> Presage the downfall of my empery,
> Nor blazing comets threaten Dido's death;
> It is Aeneas' frown that ends my days
> If he forsake me not, I never die;
> For in his looks I see eternity,
> And he'll make me immortal with a kiss.

Dido's monologue is active because she moves through eight active moments that build on one another:

- She praises (the natural world);
- She wishes (Aeneas would never leave);
- She decides (to keep him from leaving at all costs);
- She plans (how to keep him);
- She sends servants out (to execute her plan);
- She reflects (on how unhappy keeping him here will make him);
- She decides (that his being unhappy is better than her killing herself because he has left her); and
- She decides (they are meant to be together forever).

These moments culminate in her re-committing herself to force Aeneas to stay with her, which changes the trajectory of the play.

> ### Fun Fact
>
> Thespians: Sometimes, theatre artists are called "Thespians." The word comes from the name of the ancient Greek poet and performer Thespis. In Ancient Greece, plays were entirely spoken by groups of performers – called a chorus – until Thespis stepped out of the chorus to speak individual monologues. So, an individual theatre artist is called a "Thespian."

Another way to activate a monologue: give the character a realization* that has the potential to change their lives.

For example, the monologue "My Teacher" from the play *The Third Eye,* created by The National Theatre of the Deaf Ensemble, explores a harmful misconception by a teacher. The monologue is active because the character has a realization then contemplates changing based on that realization.

For this monologue, it's important to know that this character is Deaf (the audience learns this information earlier in the play):

FREDA/CAROL

A teacher said to me, "Teaching the deaf children through the means of speech training is the best method to adopt because: the majority is hearing and it is up to the minority like you to join them. Being able to speak is likely to help you people be accepted into the world."

So, I spend my life learning to be like the others and I can speak and read lips. And I wonder, now, how valuable it is that we must always try to be like others. My deafness is . . . myself. Must it be something that I must fight against, or hide, or overcome?[2]

In addition to being an active monologue, let's notice that its specificity makes this monologue universal. While audience members are not all Deaf, they relate to being told something about themselves by an authority figure that made them feel bad or wrong.

As you write, you'll discover many different ways to activate monologues.

A soliloquy is one form of monologue. In a soliloquy, a character speaks to themselves out loud, usually to make a decision.

For example, in playwright Euripides' *Medea* (400s BC), Medea is debating whether or not to kill her own children to spare them from the torture of living in a dangerous world where they are destined for pain and suffering.

At the beginning of this section of the soliloquy, she rages against the feeling that she must kill her children to spare them:

MEDEA
Ah, Ah, thou Wrath within me! Do not thou,

> Do not. . . . Down, down, thou tortured thing,
> and spare
> My children! They will dwell with us, aye, there
> Far off, and give thee peace.

But then she realizes that it's too late; fate has decreed that her children should suffer. It is better to keep them from suffering by killing them without pain herself:

> Too late, too late!
> By all Hell's living agonies of hate,
> They shall not take my little ones alive
> To make their mock with! Howsoe'er I strive
> The thing is doomed; it shall not escape now
> From being. Aye, the crown is on the brow,
> And the robe girt, and in the robe that high
> Queen dying . . .
> Come, children; stand
> A little from me. There. Reach out your hand,
> Your right hand – so – to mother: and good-bye!

In the next moment of the play, she murders her children.

Writing Exercise with Optional Group Component

Select one of the characters that you've created through writing exercises earlier in this chapter.

Now, answer these questions:

- What does she obsess about?
- What has she never accomplished that she wanted to?

- What does she secretly want that she could never say out loud?

Select one answer from the list.

Write a monologue where your character admits these private thoughts to another character (seen or unseen, soliloquies are welcome).

Now, read the monologue aloud. What did you learn from externalizing these private, internal thoughts? Who were they speaking to? Why are they important to your character? What is their relationship to your character?

Now, revise and then read the monologue aloud to someone else. Then, ask them what they learned about your character. This will help you know what information about your character is successfully communicated to your audience.

You can use what you learn through writing monologues as building blocks for your play.

Overview

Monologues are speeches or stories given by a single character. They are active – meaning that they are trying to do something, not just imparting information.

Check-In

If writing a play as you move through this book, then make sure you've created at least four characters by this point. You may feel the characters belong in one play or different plays. For now, just focus on selecting characters you are excited to explore. At least two of these characters should be in opposition to one another.

Resources
Student Favorites

The plays listed here were some of my students' favorites for illustrating the lessons in this chapter.

- *The Crucible* by Arthur Miller (Penguin Classics)
  - In the rigid theocracy of 17th-century Salem, rumors that women are practicing witchcraft galvanize the town's most basic fears and suspicions. It uses history to provoke conversations about the destructive power of socially sanctioned violence.

- *Electricidad* by Luis Alfaro (*The Greek Trilogy by Luis Alfaro*/Methuen)
  - Based on Sophocles' *Electra*, this play transplants themes of the ancient Greek tragedy on the 21st-century streets of Los Angeles.

Additional Resource

- *The Monologue Project* (tools for educators): folger. edu/teach/resource/the-monologue-project/ (Folger Shakespeare Library)

Discussed in Chapter

- *The Glass Menagerie* by Tennessee Williams (New Directions)
- *Medea* by Euripides (translated by Gilbert Murray/ Project Gutenberg/eBook #35451)
- *My Third Eye* by The National Theatre of the Deaf Ensemble (*Plays of Our Own*/Routledge)
- *The Tragedy of Dido Queene of Carthage* by Christopher Marlowe (Project Gutenberg/eBook #16169)

Notes

1 *The Glass Menagerie* by Tennessee Williams, New Directions; Some Pages Turned Down, Name on Side edition, 1999.
2 *Plays of Our Own: An Anthology of Scripts by Deaf and Hard-of-Hearing Writers*, The National Theatre of the Deaf Ensemble (Dave Berman, Linda Bove, Bernard Bragg, Carol Flemming, Patrick Graybill, Richard Kendall, Dorothy Miles, Mary Beth Miller, Fredricka Norman, Joseph Sarpy, Timothy Scanlon, Kenneth Swiger, and Edmund Waterstreet), Edited by Willy Conley, Routledge, 2023.

5
Conflict and Action

Conflict and Action are important elements of playwriting that demand a significant amount of attention from the playwright.

Scene Work

In this chapter, we'll begin writing exercises that ask that you write scenes. Later in the book, we'll dissect the specifics of how a scene works. For now, we're using the word "scene" very loosely; write what feels right to you. You simply need to generate more material for us to use as a starting place for future exercises.

Conflict

Conflict means to be in opposition to something, person, or idea.

In theatre, three primary ways that we externalize conflict are:

- Characters in conflict with one another.
- A character struggling with something inside themselves.
- A character in conflict with the larger world around them (culture, idea, society).

DOI: 10.4324/9781003505310-7

Conflicts are externalized so that the audience can perceive them.

Going Beyond "Yes" and "No"

In first drafts, as we are still learning about the characters and their world, many of our conflicts are straightforward "yes/no" arguments. One character says, "I want to do this thing." The other character says, "No, you can't do that thing." One character says, "Yes." The other says, "No." This is the surface of the play. We must dig deeper to discover the roots of the "yes/no" and what it means to the characters and their world. Then, we revise to bring that deeper conflict to the stage.

An example of a "yes/no" conflict that goes beyond a verbal tug-of-war is found in playwright Wole Soyinka's *Death and the King's Horseman.* In the play, Elesin is a King's Horseman in Nigeria who follows local Yoruba traditions. These traditions require that he commit suicide after the King's death to help the King ascend to the afterlife and to preserve his family's honor. But Elesin is prevented from committing suicide by Simon, the British colonial authority, who says suicide is illegal under colonial rule.

Throughout the play, Elesin and Simon hold opposing views, but the conflict goes much deeper than conversations where they argue: "Yes, I will do this./No, you will not."

To show his opposition to the ritual, Simon physically stops the ritual from occurring. The result for Elesin's community is catastrophic. There are fighting and recriminations, personal consequences (like Elesin losing social status), and communal consequences (the well-being of the community is in doubt). There is a concern that the universe itself is now unbalanced because the ritual has been interrupted. Later, Elesin's son returns and commits suicide to restore his family's honor and return balance to the universe.

In order to create the conflicts and actions in this play, Soyinka had to know about the backgrounds of his characters, their wants, desires, and social expectations. How the characters respond to the conflicts – and how they choose to take action– is rooted in their cultural backgrounds and beliefs. Soyinka's knowledge of his characters and their world gave him the information he needed to move the conflict beyond a "yes/no" conversation.

This is one reason digging deep into your character's history, culture, and backstory is so important; you gain vital knowledge which allows you to write a more powerful play.

Writing Exercise

This writing exercise helps you learn how to deepen a conflict between two characters, getting them to move beyond just saying "yes" and "no" to one another.

Select a character you created in an earlier writing exercise.

What would they want to do on a weekend afternoon? (e.g., nap, exercise, go roller skating)

Now, write a scene where the first character wants to do the activity, but a second character arrives who does not want to do the activity. They engage in a "yes/no" conversation.

Next, step back. What did you learn about each of these characters?

Revise the scene using something you learned about the characters to push the conflict beyond a "yes/no" conversation by including a non-verbal externalized moment.

As you move into the next series of writing exercises, be more aware of creating conflicts between your characters that go beyond having a "yes/no" conversation.

Overview

Conflicts in theatre move beyond "yes/no" conversations to deeper questions about individuals, cultures, and societies.

Size of Conflicts

Conflicts come in many shapes and sizes. The conflict is the "right" size when it's based on something the character cares deeply about – whether that is walking across a room or saving someone's life.

Conflicts can appear to be small.

For example, a person tries to carry a chair across a windy room, but the wind keeps blowing them back into a corner. We watch as the person struggles against the wind, changes tactics, and eventually makes it to the other side. We wonder: Will they make it across? Is the wind symbolic*? Is this piece really about human's place in the universe and their relationship with nature?

Conflict can appear to be everyday actions.

For example, in *Cinderella*, Cinderella wants to go to the ball, which signifies her growth into adulthood, but her Stepmother does not want her to go. We wonder: Will Cinderella ever reach the ball? Will she rebel against her family and come of age as a young woman in her society, or will she stay at home and remain a child?

Conflicts can appear to be large.

For example, in *Little Red Riding Hood*, Little Red and her grandmother need to escape the Big Bad Wolf, or they will lose their lives. We wonder: Will they escape? Or will they die? Can families survive the worst together and thrive, or will a dangerous individual destroy their love?

The playwright determines the size of the conflict based on the needs of the play. What's important is that the character is invested in that conflict.

Overview

The size of the conflict can vary based on the needs of the play. Regardless of the size of the conflict, it should be a conflict that deeply impacts the character.

Fun Fact

The Curse of Macbeth: Saying "Macbeth" in a theatre is bad luck. Instead, inside a theatre, artists call it "The Scottish Play." According to legend, the actor playing Lady Macbeth in the first-ever performance of the play died suddenly, meaning Shakespeare himself had to play the role. In following performances, other artists died both onstage and offstage while performing in the play. The play was said to be cursed, so no one uses the actual name of the play within a theatre itself.

Action

"Action" means a process of doing something that holds meaning for the character, the world of the play, and/or the audience.

These processes can be physical, but they are also emotional, spiritual, or other interior (unseen) actions that we externalize for the audience.

Often, people think of "action" as one physical thing; for example, he jumps on a chair. But action in theatre means both the physical action – jumping on a chair – as well as the interior (unseen) actions – the conflict that caused him to jump on the chair, the emotional response before jumping on the chair that evolves into how he feels while standing on the chair.

We see a clear example of action in playwright Desi Moreno-Penson's dark comedy *Devil land*. In the play, Beatriz can't have a child so she kidnaps one and locks her in the basement. Beatriz's husband Americo chains up the child, Destiny, so the girl can't escape during dinner:

[Lights up. BEATRIZ is now seated at the kitchenette table along with DESTINY (a child character played by an adult actress). Beatriz is noticeably nervous. Her husband AMERICO is adjusting and fiddling with a chain attached to a pipe and is fixing a shackle around DESTINY'S ankle.]

BEATRIZ
(*to AMERICO; irritated*) Aren't you finished yet?
AMERICO
Just give me a second.
BEATRIZ
You've been there for an hour.
AMERICO
Will you relax?
BEATRIZ
She hasn't eaten today, and the soup is getting cold.
AMERICO
Then go ahead and EAT . . .! God . . . what the fuck is wrong with you?

BEATRIZ

No, don't do that. Don't use God and fuck in the same sentence.

DESTINY

I'm not hungry.

BEATRIZ

(*brightly to her*) It doesn't matter, honey. You have to eat something. (*To AMERICO; irritated*) The tenants will hear that noise –

AMERICO

So what?

DESTINY

They'll think it's a ghost.

AMERICO

(*chuckles*) Yeah, there you go . . .!

BEATRIZ

I didn't say that.

DESTINY

But they will. The people . . . when they hear the chain rattling . . . they'll think it's a ghost. And they'll say the building's on top of an Indian burial ground. I saw that in a movie.

AMERICO

Indian ghosts in the Bronx? (*Laughs*)

BEATRIZ

Don't laugh at her.

DESTINY

(*nods*) Uh-huh . . . we're Indians, right? Mami says we all come from Caribbean Indians in Puerto Rico.

BEATRIZ

That's a different kind of Indian.

DESTINY
And those Indians are called Tainos.

BEATRIZ
But we're not Tainos anymore, honey –

AMERICO
(*with one final tug on the chain*) Okay, this should hold.

BEATRIZ
We're civilized people now.

DESTINY
(*seeing the soup tureen and bowls*) Are we going to eat?

BEATRIZ
Yes, we're all going to sit down and eat. Together.

DESTINY
It's too hot in here to eat.

BEATRIZ
(*serving her*) I know. But you need to eat something.
Come sit down.

DESTINY
I can't. It's too hot.

BEATRIZ
Try. I want you to try.

DESTINY
I can't.

BEATRIZ
You can.

AMERICO
Don't force her.

BEATRIZ
I'm not going to let her starve herself in front of me. (*A pause*) Bless us, Oh Lord, for these, thy gifts, that we are about to receive from thy bounty. Amen.[1]

As we see in the above scene between Americo, Beatriz, and Destiny, there are multiple actions happening in this scene:

- The physical action of chaining up Destiny.
- The physical action of serving and eating dinner.
- The verbal action of conflict between Americo and Beatriz.
- The verbal action of conflict between Beatriz and Destiny.
- Later, we'll learn that the discussion of Tainos is part of greater conflict over the meaning of culture within the play.

Action is a dynamic, ongoing, multi-layered process.

In early drafts, your theatrical moments might only have one layer of action because you are still figuring out your play. However, as you move through the revision process, you'll begin expanding, shifting, and overlapping actions which adds depth and meaning to your play.

Writing Exercise

Creating layers of action is an important skill for a playwright.

- Take a character you've created.
- Pick a physical action that's meaningful for them (e.g., painting to relax, hugging their child).
- Write a short scene where they do that action.
- Now, insert another character into the scene. That character is mocking that physical action in words and/or movement.

- How does the first character respond to being mocked in words? What do they say?
- What intellectual ideas come to mind? What sharp emotional responses?
- Think about the layers of response – physical, emotional, and intellectual – that are driven by being mocked for something that is meaningful to them. Add those responses to the scene when you revise.

As you evolve as a playwright, you'll learn how to build more complex and engaging actions.

Overview

In plays, "action" means a process of doing something that holds meaning for the character, the world of the play, and/or the audience. These processes can be physical, but they are also emotional, spiritual, or other interior (unseen) actions that we externalize for the audience. Action is a dynamic, ongoing process.

Conflict Leads to Action

Conflict leads to action in a play. These conflicts evolve over the course of the play; so, a conflict leads to an action, which then leads to another conflict, which leads to another action, and so on for the length of the play.

Let's look at two examples from earlier in this chapter:

- In *Cinderella,* when Cinderella is forbidden to attend the ball (conflict), she makes a decision to go anyway (action). Once she decides to go, she needs to make a dress for the ball (action). She uses dress material without permission which angers her family (conflict).
- In *Little Red Riding Hood,* the Wolf chases the Grandmother (conflict), then Grandmother hides in the clock where the Wolf cannot reach her (action), so the Wolf decides to dress up as Grandmother (action) to fool Little Red into coming close to him so he can try to eat her (conflict).

Often, conflict makes a character act. However, sometimes, conflict leads to a character refusing to act even in the face of enormous consequences – and that it itself – an active refusal to change – is action.

Sometimes, multiple conflicts and actions will be layered on top of one another.

In the following excerpt from playwright Kālidāsa's *Shakuntala* (4th century) King Dushyanta and his companion Clown Madhavya are on a hunting trip. But the Clown is tired of hunting. So, the Clown fakes an injury to get the King to rest for a day. The King agrees to rest. But, in exchange, the King wants help pursuing the beautiful Shakuntala.

Also, in order to rest for a day, the Clown and the King face a smaller conflict with the General, who wishes to continue without a break.

So, we have the larger conflict between the Clown and the King. Within that conflict, another conflict occurs between the King and the General. The conflict between the King and the General must be resolved before the conflict between the Clown and the King can be resolved.

Once both of those conflicts are resolved, then that resolution leads to the next action of the play: pursuing Shakuntala. So, the resolution of both conflicts propels them into the next action.

In this scene, the Clown fakes an injury on the hunting trip:

Clown (*standing as before*). Well, king, I can't move my
    hand. I can only greet you with my voice.
King (*looking and smiling*). What makes you lame?
Clown You hit a man in the eye, and then ask him why
    the tears come.
King I do not understand you. Speak plainly.
Clown When a reed bends over like a hunchback, do
    you blame the reed or the river-current?
King The river-current, of course.
Clown And you are to blame for my troubles.
King How so?
Clown Here I am, a Brahman, and my joints are all
    shaken up by this eternal running after wild animals,
    so that I can't move. Please be good to me. Let us
    have a rest for just one day.
King (*to himself*). He says this. And I too, when
    I remember Kanva's daughter [Shakuntala], have
    little desire for the chase. For

> The bow is strung, its arrow near;
> And yet I cannot bend
> That bow against the fawns who share
> Soft glances with their friend.

Clown (*observing the king*). He means more than he says. I might as well weep in the woods.

King (*smiling*). What more could I mean? I have been thinking that I ought to take my friend's advice.

Clown (*cheerfully*). Long life to you, then.

King Wait. Hear me out.

Clown Well, sir?

King You must be my companion in another task – an easy one.

Clown Crushing a few sweetmeats?

King I will tell you presently.

Clown Pray command my leisure.

[The King summons the General.]

General (*to himself*). Hunting is declared to be a sin, yet it brings nothing but good to the king. See!

> He does not heed the cruel sting
> Of his recoiling, twanging string;
> The mid-day sun, the dripping sweat
> Affect him not, nor make him fret;
> His form, though sinewy and spare,
> Is most symmetrically fair;
> No mountain-elephant could be
> More filled with vital strength than he.

(*He approaches*) Victory to your Majesty! The forest is full of deer-tracks, and beasts of prey cannot be far off. What better occupation could we have?

King Bhadrasena [General], my enthusiasm is broken. Madhavya [the Clown] has been preaching against hunting.

General (aside to the clown). Stick to it, friend Madhavya. I will humour the king a moment. (*Aloud.*) Your Majesty, he is a chattering idiot. Your Majesty may judge by his own case whether hunting is an evil. Consider:

> The hunter's form grows sinewy, strong, and light;
> He learns, from beasts of prey, how wrath and fright
> Affect the mind; his skill he loves to measure
> With moving targets. 'Tis life's chiefest pleasure.

Clown (angrily). Get out! Get out with your strenuous life! The king has come to his senses. But you can go chasing from forest to forest, till you fall into the jaws of some old bear that is looking for a deer or a jackal.

King [General] I cannot take your advice, because I am in the vicinity of a hermitage. So for to-day

> The hornèd buffalo may shake
> The turbid water of the lake;
> Shade-seeking deer may chew the cud,
> Boars trample swamp-grass in the mud;
> The bow I bend in hunting, may
> Enjoy a listless holiday.

General Yes, your Majesty.

King Send back the archers who have gone ahead. And forbid the soldiers to vex the hermitage, or even to approach it. Remember:

> There lurks a hidden fire in each
> Religious hermit-bower;

Cool sun-stones kindle if assailed

By any foreign power.

General Yes, your Majesty.

Clown Now will you get out with your strenuous life?
   (*Exit general.*)

King (*to his attendants.*) Lay aside your hunting dress.

Clown Now be seated on this flat stone, over which the
   trees spread their canopy of shade. I can't sit down
   till you do.

King Lead the way.

Clown Follow me. (*They walk about and sit down.*)

King Friend Madhavya, you do not know what vision
   is. You have not seen the fairest of all objects.

Clown I see you, right in front of me.

King Yes, everyone thinks himself beautiful. But I was
   speaking of Shakuntala, the ornament of the hermitage.

Clown (*to himself*). I mustn't add fuel to the flame.
   (*Aloud.*) But you can't have her because she is a
   hermit-girl. What is the use of seeing her?

King Fool!

      And is it selfish longing then,

      That draws our souls on high

      Through eyes that have forgot to wink,

      As the new moon climbs the sky?

Besides, [my] thoughts dwell on no forbidden object.

Clown Well, tell me about her.

King

      Sprung from a nymph of heaven

      Wanton and gay,

      Who spurned the blessing given,

      Going her way;

> By the stern hermit taken
> In her most need:
> So fell the blossom shaken,
> Flower on a weed.

Clown (*laughing*.) You are like a man who gets tired
  of good dates and longs for sour tamarind. All the
  pearls of the palace are yours, and you want this girl!
King My friend, you have not seen her, or you could
  not talk so.

In this scene, we see how conflicts lead to actions. Also note, the conflicts are based in each character working to get what they "want" out of the situation. (The Clown wants to take a break from hunting. The King wants to pursue Shakuntala. The General wants to continue hunting.) Wants, conflicts, and actions work together to create an engaging scene.

Writing Exercise and Optional Group Component

Here are three writing prompts for creating a juicy moment of conflict; spend 15 minutes writing a scene based on one of these prompts:

- Kenyatta has been set up on a blind date with David. When they meet, Kenyatta is not interested in David at all. Kenyatta tries to end the date without hurting David's feelings.
- Thor and Aditi are colleagues who work in the same office. A co-worker quit, and Aditi and Thor

both want his (much nicer) desk. They both try to move into the desk at the same time.

- María has returned home. She says her child is missing, but the babysitter insists the child is still in the room.

If you are working with a group, Now, read these scenes aloud to one another. Can your audience identify the main conflict in each scene and tell you the action(s) the characters take to resolve the conflict?

In the future, be more aware of creating conflicts for, and taking actions with, your characters.

Overview

There are many forms of conflict within plays. Regardless of structure, most plays are centered around conflicts and actions.

Action and Reaction

Action is a process of doing something that holds meaning for the character, the world of the play, and/or the audience.

Reaction is what characters do in response to the action. Action and reaction lead to conflict.

For example, when Mom dies, the character might weep. Mom's death is an action. The weeping is a reaction.

A reaction can be compelling for a moment, but then it should be tied to another action. Otherwise, the reaction becomes passive and uninteresting to watch, and the audience's understanding of the character stalls.

Here is how we could turn that reaction into a sequence of actions and reactions leading to conflict:

- Action: Mom dies.
- Reaction: Character weeps.
- Action: Character calls Dad and offers to pay for a funeral.
- Reaction: Dad is surprised.
- Action: Dad says, "No, I'm going to dump her body in the backyard."
- Reaction: Character is horrified and angry.
- Action: Character says, "You are not going to throw her in the backyard. That's terrible!"
- Reaction: Dad says, "It's the right thing to do."
- Conflict: Character and Dad now must battle it out over who gets to bury Mom's body and how it will be done.

Action, reaction, and conflict based on a character's "wants" build on one another throughout a play.

Sometimes, artists will refer to one action as a "beat*" – as in we go from the "beat" where Mom dies to the "beat" where the Character weeps. However, artists use the word "beat" in different ways so make sure to clarify with your collaborators how they are using the word.

Overview

Make sure your characters act – and not just react – to what is happening to them.

Resources
Student Favorites

The plays listed here were some of my students' favorites for illustrating the lessons in this chapter.

- *The Cake* by Bekah Brunstetter (Concord Theatricals)
  - Della makes cakes, not judgment calls but when the girl she helped raise comes back home to North Carolina to get married to a woman, Della's life gets turned upside down. A comedy that asks: who gets to decide who you are allowed to love?

- *Caught* by Christopher Chen (Dramatists Play Service)
  - An art gallery hosts a retrospective of the work of a dissident artist who was imprisoned in a Chinese detention center. An exploration of truth, art, social justice, and cultural appropriation.

Additional Resource

- The *How to Playwright podcast* by playwright Lauren M. Gunderson (America's most-produced playwright) explores narrative playwriting popular in the United States. (all major podcast outlets)

Discussed in Chapter

- *Cinderella* based on Charles Perrault's folktale (Disney film, 1950)
- *Little Red Riding Hood* based on a folktale by Valentina and Zinaida Semyonovna Brumberg (1937 short film(youtu.be/xb2vD2ovqE8?si=5rZi-WRreIB8ssQo)
- *Death and the King's Horseman* by Wole Soyinka (W.W. Norton)
- *Devil Land* by Desi Moreno-Penson (Broadway Play Publishing)
- *Shakuntala* by Kālidāsa's (translated by Arthur W. Ryder, *Shakuntala and Other Works*/Project Gutenberg/eBook #16659)

Note
1 *Devil Land* by Desi Moreno-Penson, Broadway Play Publishing, 2011.

6
Dialogue

Dialogue and stage directions are the main two ways that playwrights communicate action and conflict on the page.

Dialogue

Dialogue is a character's words that are externally communicated. For example, they might be spoken or projected onto a screen.

In dialogue, every character speaks the public language(s) of their community; this is the language of their everyday life in public. For example, as a person from the Deep South in the U.S., I say, "How are you?" in English when greeting my neighbor.

How a character speaks that public language is informed by their personal experiences, race, class, geographical region, education level, and other factors. Two characters may speak the same public language – for example, English – but the way those characters speak that language is different based on their circumstances in the world – for example, as a greeting do they say "Hello," "Hi," "Hey," or "What's up"?

 DOI: 10.4324/9781003505310-8

For example, let's say a line of dialogue in proper English is "Get the dogs into the house." If I write a character from the rural American South, I'd write, "Get 'em back in that house." But if I write a character in a Shakespeare-inspired play, I'd write, "Get thee to thine home, you damnable beast."

Overview

Dialogue is a character's words and reflects that character's community, background, and experience.

Grammar

Dialogue does not have to be grammatically correct; how a character speaks tells us as much about them as what they say.

For example, if a character is threatening someone, then *how* they threaten the person tells us a lot about the character. If someone is confident in their threat, then they might say: "I'm going to beat you to a bloody pulp!" But if someone is less confident in their threat, then they might say: "You better, better not, I mean . . . I'm going to beat you up . . . or something. If you don't, leave, or, or, something."

The way a character speaks is one way of showing, of externalizing, what is happening emotionally inside themselves.

Overview

Dialogue does not have to be grammatically correct. Dialogue should reflect the individual character and their particular state in that moment.

Punctuation

Punctuation is an important indicator of how a line should be spoken and the meaning behind it.

For example, if a couple is fighting, and a woman is angry, then her dialogue might be:

HER: I. Can. Not. Stand. You! Anymore! Get out!

But if she's only annoyed, her dialogue might be:

HER: Pu-leaze. I cannot stand you anymore. Go away.

But if she's incredibly angry, her dialogue might be:

HER: Icannotstandyouanymore!Icannotstandyouanym ore! Icannotstandyouanymore!Icannotstandyouany more! Leave! NOW!

Writing Exercise and Optional Group Exercise

Punctuation in dialogue can help express the underlying emotions and meaning of the words.

Open a play and write down the first four to six lines of dialogue that you see as it is written on the page.

Now, take those same lines and change the punctuation. What happens if you add exclamation and question marks? What changes if you remove all of the periods? Play with different ways of using punctuation and think about how it changes the emotions and meaning of the exchange. (Do not worry about the context of the lines in the original play. This is just an exercise.)

If you are working with a group, give someone the original lines as well as one set of differently punctuated lines. Have them read the original and the new version. Discuss how this changes the lines of dialogue and what different meanings, emotions, or stories emerge.

Playwrights use punctuation to indicate how a line is communicated.

In other instances, playwrights remove punctuation to express the flowing nature of the work and how it should move onstage.

In playwright Celine Song's *Endlings,* the first act moves between two locations: Man-Jae Island in Korea and the East Village, New York City. Song writes the first act with almost no punctuation. Her lack of punctuation and the way the words are allowed to flow freely across the page gives readers a feeling of the fluid nature of the piece which flows seamlessly between different locations, characters, and ideas. This choice to use very little punctuation helps readers of the script understand how it should be performed on the stage.

Plays are living documents. Punctuation can help show on the page, how the play should move on the stage.

Occasionally, playwrights will include a short indicator of how a character is feeling in parenthesis for clarity. For example:

HER: (*sarcastic*) I love you.

Use these sparingly. Usually, when you need many parentheticals, it means that the dialogue is weak and cannot carry the play.

How you present your text on the page will evolve as your play evolves throughout writing, revisions, and productions*.

And, yes, playwrights continue to revise between productions! Playwrights often learn new things about the play in production, which leads to them revising the play on the page before the next production.

In a famous case of revision between productions, playwright Richard Brinsley Sheridan of the comedy *The School for Scandal* – a witty and pointed depiction of the ridiculousness of high society – opened the play in January of 1775, but people hated it, so they immediately closed the show. Then he rewrote and recast the comedy in 11 days. It re-opened, and the new version of the show was a hit! It launched his career. But it took seeing the play onstage in production with an audience to know what was working and what wasn't.

Writing Exercise

Make a list of ten people that you know; for example, an account manager in an office, a pet store owner, a six-year-old child.

Select two of the characters.

They do not know one another. They each have a golden retriever that has gotten loose and run away. They both see a golden retriever, think it is their own, and collide. They argue over whether or not the dog is their own. As they argue, the dog runs away again.

Now, write a short narrative description of the characters and why each character is in the park.

Go back to your scene and revise with all of this information in mind; is one character running late from work and so frazzled, and that contributes to the fight? Is one character a math teacher who tries to use math terms to explain their position?

Part of playwriting is getting comfortable learning more about your characters as you go and implementing that knowledge. Writing is revision.

To learn more about how to format your dialogue on the page, see Appendix A.

Overview

As you write, you'll learn more about your character, which will help you write more specific dialogue for them. The act of refining a character's voice through their dialogue continues throughout the writing process.

Thoughts on Writing Dialogue from playwright Kate Tarker of Montag:

You know that sweet children's rhyme, "Sticks and stones may break my bones, but words shall never hurt me?" The opposite is true on stage. Words are all-powerful here. Speech is typically the primary way characters seek to negotiate change in their lives, in their relationships, in their understanding of the world. Speech can change everything between people. To that end, you want to supercharge your characters' speech with intention*, rhythm, and direction (they're always speaking *to* someone).

To get my mind into dialogue mode, I sometimes visualize each of my characters' utterances as physical objects that they will have to intentionally pick up and throw across the stage toward their recipient.

For example, I'll annotate a purely verbal exchange from my play *Montag*. Novella verbally offers her friend Faith a potato chip. She says, "Chip?" like she's tossing an actual chip across the table that hits Faith in her blouse. "I can't eat that shit," says Faith, as if pulling the chip back out of her cleavage and throwing the chip back at her friend, hard. "Why not?" asks Novella, undeterred, like she's tossing two fresh chips across the table. "I get heartburn," says Faith, as if she's smashing the new chips with her fist, and then sliding them back across the table. "What the hell is that?" asks Novella, as if picking the crumbs back off the table and pouring them into her mouth. In the context of the play, the women are really arguing about something much bigger and more serious than potato chips, but the conflict infuses every word they say.

Even fragments of speech can leave a lasting imprint. Of course, this truth is embedded in that schoolyard rhyme too. If there's charged speech whizzing your way, immediately fight back with a verbal counter-spell. Otherwise, those words just might crack you open.[1]

Dialogue and a Character's Point of View

A character's point of view is revealed through dialogue.

For example, let's pretend we're trying to express that a duck has turned blue. Here are a few dialogue options:

- A Child: I love blue ducks!
- A Cranky Person: Ugh, just one more thing to go wrong today, the duck turned blue!
- A Dreamer: What a sign of wonderful things to come, the duck turning blue.
- A Fastidious Person: I abhor when a perfectly elegant white duck turns that dreadful shade of blue.
- A Fellow Duck: Hey! Ronald's blue. Think he's sick or just showing off again?

The character's perspective shapes their dialogue. Then, those perspectives shape a character's actions.

For example, the Child who is excited by the blue duck tries to pet him. The Dreamer who thinks the duck is a good sign buys a lottery ticket. The Fellow Duck who is annoyed swims away from him.

Dialogue, grammar, punctuation, and point of view work together to communicate the moment which leads to actions. Those actions will lead to more conflicts, and the play continues moving forward.

Writing Exercise

Pretend you are writing a play where a birthday cake burns in the oven. Write dialogue that reflects this from different perspectives and different emotions. Begin by writing a few lines from each of these perspectives:

- The Baker who worked very hard on the cake and is upset that it is burnt.
- The Friend who tries to make the Baker feel better about the cake burning.
- The Baker's sibling who makes fun of the Baker baking the cake.

Now, think of one more character who might be in the scene, and write lines from their perspective.

Playwrights work to infuse dialogue with a character's point of view.

Characters also change the way they speak depending on who they are speaking to and what is going on around them.

For example, let's say my character is in a scene and doesn't want a sandwich. If their sister offers them a sandwich at home, then they'd say, "Yeah, I find ham and cheese sandwiches so gross." But if their boss offers them a sandwich at the office, they'd say, "No, Ma'am, I don't need a sandwich today, but thank you for offering."

Overview

A character's dialogue is shaped by many influences, including their background, their perspective on the situation, their emotional state, and the location where the dialogue is spoken.

Writing Exercise and Optional Group Exercise

Let's practice changing a piece of dialogue based on the context around it. One person turns to another and expresses that there is a bad smell in the air. How would they share this information if they were:

- In a fancy restaurant.
- At a baseball stadium.
- At home in bed with your partner.

Now, write three more lines based on other locations.

If you are working with a group, read one of your first three lines aloud, but don't tell them the location. Can they tell – just from the line itself – the type of location your character inhabits? Discuss.

Context shapes dialogue in a play.

All Dialogue is Stylized Dialogue

Emerging writers sometimes worry that their dialogue does not sound "real" enough. Do not worry. All dialogue is stylizing dialogue. All dialogue has a certain style because it is generated by an artist who is shaping it. It is defined by the parameters of the piece (you are choosing what to leave in and leave out) and your subjective point of view.

Even if you are creating documentary theatre – theatre that uses interviews and other direct accounts – it can be argued that since the real person's dialogue is edited and reinterpreted by a performer, it is also stylized because it is being shaped by the hand of the artist.

So, don't worry about making your dialogue "real" in terms of how people speak in everyday life. Instead, focus on writing strong dialogue that makes sense for your characters and the world they inhabit.

Playwright August Wilson of *The Piano Lesson* said,

> My early attempts writing plays, which are very poetic, did not use the language that I work in now. I didn't recognize the poetry in everyday language of Black America.[2]

Later in his writing journey, he embraced the poetry of the everyday and then shaped it to make sense for his characters and their theatrical worlds.

For example, in Act One of *The Piano Lesson*, Berniece talks about the importance of the piano to their mother and, by extension, their family story. She could have just said, "This piano is important to Mom. You know that. It's carried our family story with it." That still would be slightly stylized, but it would not encompass the rich feeling of the world or the passion of the character. Instead, Wilson writes Berneice's line as:

> Look at this piano. Look at it. Mama Ola polished this piano with her tears for seventeen years. For seventeen years she rubbed on it till her hands bled. Then she rubbed the blood in . . . mixed it up with the rest of the blood on it.[3]

Wilson's dialogue is so effective because it is stylized to emphasize and expand upon the intrinsic "poetry in the everyday language of Black America."

An example of more overtly stylized dialogue can be found in playwright Edna St. Vincent Millay's comedy *Aria Da Capo*. In this scene, Millay showcases her characters flamboyant comic style while eating dinner:

COLUMBINE: Pierrot, a macaroon! I cannot live
   without a macaroon!
PIERROT: My only love, You are so intense! . . . Is it
   Tuesday, Columbine? – I'll kiss you if it's Tuesday.
COLUMBINE: It is Wednesday, If you must know
   . . . . Is this my artichoke, Or yours?
PIERROT: Ah, Columbine, – as if it mattered!
   Wednesday . . . . Will it be Tuesday, then, to-
   morrow, By any chance?
COLUMBINE: To-morrow will be – Pierrot, That isn't
   funny!

PIERROT: I thought it rather nice. Well, let us
    drink some wine and lose our heads And love
    each other.
COLUMBINE: Pierrot, don't you love Me now?
PIERROT: La, what a woman! – how should I know?
    Pour me some wine: I'll tell you presently.
COLUMBINE: Pierrot, do you know, I think you
    drink too much.
PIERROT: Yes, I dare say I do. . . . Or else too little.
    It's hard to tell. You see, I am always wanting
    A little more than what I have, – or else A little less.
    There's something wrong. My dear, How many
    fingers have you?
COLUMBINE: La, indeed, How should I know? – It
    always takes me one hand To count the other with.
    It's too confusing.

Both Wilson and Millay write dialogue that works beautifully within the context of their plays. The dialogue is right for the characters and their worlds.

Overview

Focus on writing dialogue that feels true to your specific character in their specific situation. Your dialogue will evolve as your characters grow and change and you become a stronger writer.

Check-In

If writing a play as you move through this book, then begin to get a feel for your character's voices. If you need more exercises than are available in this chapter, return to the Prologue and do some of those writing prompts as well. You don't need to know their exact voice yet, but get a sense of how they speak and how your characters sound different on the page.

Resources

Student Favorites

The plays listed here were some of my students' favorites for illustrating the lessons in this chapter. In workshops, we read scenes from each of these plays and then discuss the different approaches to dialogue. For homework, each student selects one play to read in full and writes a scene in the style of that dialogue.

- *Amadeus* by Peter Shaffer (Perennial)
  - Period-ish language.
- *Eurydice* by Sarah Ruhl (Methuen)
  - Flowing, highly poetic language and imagery.
- *Glengarry Glen Ross* by David Mamet (Grove Press)
  - Tense, taut language.

- *Milk Like Sugar* by Kirsten Greenidge (Concord Theatricals)
  - Realistic-ish language.
- *Nine Parts of Desire* by Heather Raffo (Northwestern University Press)
  - One-person show featuring multiple characters with distinct dialogue.
- *Revolt. She Said. Revolt Again.* by Alice Birch (Soho Rep/On Stage Press)
  - Short lines. Some characters are not assigned. Flexible staging/imagery.
- *Suicide Forest* by Kristine Haruna Lee (53rd State Press)
  - Multi-lingual dialogue. Performers alternate between characters and themselves as performers using different language for each.
- *The Two Kids Who Blow Shit Up* by Carla Ching (Theatrical Rights Worldwide)
  - The same character's voices shift at different ages, depending upon where they are in their personal development.

Additional Resource

- Playwrights on dialogue: youtu.be/NnLRV-ru95Y?si=hlrEOGRpNIiN6ViX (National Theatre/London)

Discussed in Chapter

- *Aria da Capo* by Edna St. Vincent Millay (Project Gutenberg/eBook #5790)
- *Endlings* by Celine Song (Theatrical Rights Worldwide Plays)
- *Montag* by Kate Tarker (Soho Rep Press)
- *The Piano Lesson* by August Wilson (Theatre Communications Group)
- *The School for Scandal* by Richard Brinsley Sheridan (Project Gutenberg/eBook #1929)

Notes

1 Printed with permission of playwright, 2024.
2 August Wilson, "The Art of Theater No. 14," *The Paris Review*, Issue 153, Winter 1999.
3 *The Piano Lesson* by August Wilson, Printed with permission of Theatre Communications Group, 2nd part. Edition, 2007.

7

Stage Directions

Dialogue and stage directions are the main two ways that playwrights communicate action and conflict on the page.

Stage Directions

Stage directions are instructions in the play that are not usually spoken. However, occasionally, they might be spoken, projected, or otherwise shared with the audience.

Stage directions have many functions.

They can share unspoken physical movements or offer a sense of character emotions. For example:

- They collapse on the bed in tears.
- He whistles the song "Happy Birthday."
- A shadow overtakes the stage.
- Her smile disintegrates as he leaves the room.

They can describe a setting or environment, as well as objects that the playwright deems essential. For example:

- They sit in a house on the moon.
- The living room is also a boat.

 DOI: 10.4324/9781003505310-9

- The teenager holds an apple in her hand.
- The office sounds like a zoo with animal sounds in the background.

Stage directions can also clarify the overall mood or tone of a piece, especially early in the play when the audience does not yet know what's going on in the story.

For example, in my play *Bottle Fly,* I have a character whose brain was deprived of oxygen when she was being born, so she lost the ability to speak. However, she speaks directly to the audience in flowing monologues that illuminate her inner life. To make sure readers and future collaborators understand the difference between the character's outer self and inner world, I use detailed stage directions early in the play.

Warm light streams through the paper that covers the walls of the bar; the transcendent connection between K's seen and unseen worlds.

Whenever K speaks to the audience, the warm light shines through the paper, bathing her world in a transcendent glow, a visible connection of the seen and unseen worlds, a past and future perfect that contain her reality.

When we are in the realistic world of the play – where characters speak to one another in daily life but K cannot speak – the warm light disappears, and they are in the harsh fluorescent light of the bar.

Now that I have established how K transitions from the real world of the play to her inner world when she addresses the audience, I don't need to include long stage directions in future moments of transition. Now, anytime she speaks to the audience, my readers and collaborators understand what that moment should look like onstage.

Writing Exercise

Pick two of your favorite characters from literature. Now put them into a situation ripe for both physical and emotional stage directions; for example, trying to get out of a burning house, trying to avoid one another at a party, or falling in love while training for an Olympic sport.

For 15 minutes, write a scene, including all the stage directions that you can think of, for this situation.

Now, hold on to that scene. We're going to use it in the next Writing Exercise.

In early drafts, playwrights tend to overwrite stage directions. This is just us trying to draw the world and our characters clearly so that we can figure out what is going on in our play. In later drafts, stage directions tend to get clearer and more concise, or even disappear all together.

In older published plays, you'll see very specific stage directions, such as:

- Downstage* she sits on a couch and bites her nails.
- Upstage* they look curiously through a window, then climb through while rubbing their foreheads.

- Stage Right*: The right side of the stage from the actor's point of view looking out at the audience.
- Stage Left*: The left side of the stage from the actor's point of view looking out at the audience.

Today, playwrights do not typically include stage directions that are this prescriptive in their plays – so you are less likely to see notations like "downstage" or "upstage." Instead of the stage direction: "Downstage, she sits on a couch, bites her nails." You might see the stage direction: "She bites her nails nervously," which illuminates both the interior (nervous emotion) and exterior (nail-biting physicality) state of the character.

However, if describing production elements in detail helps you write the play, go for it! You can always revise them later if you wish.

Fun Fact

Stage Directions: We use the terms "downstage" (to denote the part of the stage closest to the audience) and "upstage" (to denote the part of the stage farthest from the audience) because in the early days of Western theater, some stages were built on a slope towards the audience to make it easier to see the actors. The part of the stage that was lower was closer to the audience. The part of the stage that was higher was farther from the audience. So, the actors walked down a slope "downstage" to move near the audience and walked up the slope "upstage" to move further from the audience. Even though our stages tend to be flat today, we still use these terms.

Writing Exercise with Optional Group Component

Look at the last scene you wrote. Think about which stage directions are absolutely necessary for this scene to function. What could I include in dialogue? What were stage directions that I wrote just to understand the scene for myself, which I can now edit out or pare down?

Now, edit the scene down to the minimum stage directions that you need in order for the scene to be understood.

Reflect on which stage directions you needed to clearly communicate the scene and which you thought you needed but, eventually, did not.

If you're with a group, everyone pairs off and exchange scenes. Give your partner a copy of the second scene (the one with edited-down stage directions). Read each other's scenes, then tell your partner what you think happened in their scene. Did they get to understand your intentions with fewer stage directions? Were there moments that were clear with fewer stage directions or moments that were confusing where you might need to add dialogue or stage directions to clarify?

The balance of how many stage directions and how much dialogue to use will evolve as your play develops.

Overview

Stage directions are unspoken instructions that tell us about the physical and emotional world of the characters.

What Is "Show, Don't Tell"?

People say that you should "show, don't tell" onstage. But what does that really mean? "Show, don't tell" might mean large physical action. However, more commonly, it means transmitting the experience of a moment.

For example, instead of saying, "My child is sick," a character might say, "His forehead is hotter than an oven." Or the character might touch their child's forehead, look shocked, and then pick up a thermometer.

Another example is instead of saying, "I am very cold," a character might pull out a blanket and wrap it around themselves.

The literal information is embedded in the "showing" of the moment rather than stated directly.

For example, in playwright August Strindberg's naturalistic *Miss Julie*, Miss Julie's overbearing and controlling father, the Count, is never seen. However, at the very beginning of the play, his Manservant Jean:

> *Enters [the kitchen], dressed in livery and carrying a pair of big, spurred riding-boots, which he places on the floor in such a manner that they remain visible to the spectators.*

We learn that the big, spurred riding boots belong to the Count. While we never meet the Count, his boots are prominently displayed onstage for the entire play. By centering the Count's boots with spurs on-stage – spurs being something used to kick horses to make them do what the rider wishes – the powerful presence of the domineering Count looms over them even though he is never seen. The boots remind us, and the characters, of his power. Their awareness of his power shapes the choices the characters make.

Strindberg also uses dialogue to draw a clear picture of the anger and frustration Miss Julie feels from being dominated and oppressed by the men in her life. She lashes out in a vivid monologue that shows us how she is feeling through violent imagery, which is the externalization of her violent emotions:

JULIE: . . . I'm weak, am I? I'd like to see your blood, your brains smashed on the chopping block. I want to see every one of your sex [men] swimming in a lake of blood like this one. I think I could drink out of your skull. I could wash my feet in your ripped stomach. I could roast your heart and eat. So you think I am weak?

Playwrights use a mix of dialogue and stage directions to show what is happening both internally and externally with their characters.

Stage directions can also incorporate important production elements like sound, music, and costumes which are vital to the play.

For example, in playwright Dominique Morisseau's *Detroit '67*, music plays an important role. It gives us a feel for the time period (1967) and the community (a home in a Black neighborhood in Detroit). It also helps to show the story.

Lank – a Black man – and Caroline – a white woman – dance in an increasingly sensual way to "Everybody Needs Love" by Gladys Knight and the Pips. We do not need long discussions about the time period, race, and social norms to understand that the characters are in danger because we witness them falling in love which was forbidden by society when that song was popular.[1]

Thinking About Opposition/Writing Prompt from playwright Frances Ya-Chu Cowhig of 410[Gone]:

THINKING ABOUT OPPOSITION

Opposition is a principle of theatre making that considers the various tracks of information that can be communicated to the audience in a live production, and ways these tracks can be arranged to deliver contrasting meaning. Plays are not written, they are wrought. A script is a blueprint for a time-based, three-dimensional experience. And the playwright, as architect of that dramatic experience, has the opportunity to craft their play in a way that doesn't simply deliver redundant meaning in each track.

WRITING EXERCISE

Write a scene in which there is an opposition between dialogue and stage action, between

what characters say and what they do. Or take the dialogue from a scene you have already

written and change the setting and action of the scene – modify where the characters are and what they are doing. Do this with an eye towards contrast. Try to make it absolutely necessary that your audience keeps both their eyes and ears open to understand the scene. Can they close their eyes and still understand the story? Can they plug their ears and still get it? If so, the tracks are not in opposition.[2]

"Show, don't tell" means transmitting the experience of a moment in a compelling way.

"Show, don't tell" in your play will evolve as you revise the piece.

For example, you might first write a line of dialogue like this:

> MAIN CHARACTER
> I hate my Mother, and that's why I'm not going to the Christmas party.

That line is a good place to begin. You're learning about what that character thinks and feels. Now, step back and think about how you can activate this information so it is more engaging to see onstage. A second draft of the line might be:

> (*The character speaks into the phone.*)
> MAIN CHARACTER
> No, I don't think that's right! I don't want to talk about it. I'm not going to see you for Christmas. Goodbye, Mom.
> (*The character slams down the phone, takes the turkey she's been carefully cooking for the party, and throws it into the trash can. The character turns to her roommate.*)

MAIN CHARACTER
Cancel the rental car. I can't deal with her right now.
Do you want to order take-out?

This second draft is much more interesting as it shows the Main Character's conflict with Mother.

As you continue to write the play, you'll learn more about your characters and their journeys. Then you'll take this information into your revision process. For example, the next revision could read:

> (*The main character slams down the phone, throws the carefully prepared turkey into the garbage, and grabs take-out menus.*)
> MAIN CHARACTER
> Someone must be delivering on Christmas.
> ROOMMATE
> Aren't you going to miss your Mom's party?
> CHARACTER
> The place on Park Street delivers. I'll get you a #33.

Now, the moment is more active and potent.

In addition, we get a sense of the character's relationship to their roommate because the main character clearly knows her roommate's food preferences – so they've probably known one another for a while – and feels comfortable telling the roommate what she's ordering for her – so the main character might be dominant in the relationship.

All these details contribute to how an audience perceives and understands your characters.

Writing Exercise and Optional Group Exercise

Sit in a public space. Listen to conversations occurring around you. Write them down verbatim.

Next to each sentence or fragment, write the emotion that the person is experiencing. Ignore correct grammar when you are writing down their dialogue. Instead, use words, punctuation, space on the page, and any other means to capture both the words and the feelings behind the words on the page.

Once you have the literal lines down on the paper as you want them, now play with them a bit. How would you change the lines so the emotion behind them is different? Turn an angry line into a loving one or a serious line into a funny one. Have fun!

Bring in your favorite line/collection of lines and share them with your community. Everyone picks someone else's favorite line and writes it to change the emotion behind it. Share the lines and enjoy!

Playwrights learn to show through dialogue and stage directions on the page.

Overview

"Show, don't tell" means transmitting the experience of a moment. There are many ways that transmission occurs, but all of it is underscored by conflict and action.

Subtext

Subtext is one way you "show, don't tell." Subtext is a conversation underneath the conversation the two characters are having – it's a hidden meaning that is hinted at but, for some reason, the characters cannot say directly.

The inability of the character to say their true feelings aloud is usually caused by an emotion like fear – for example, they are too afraid to say it aloud. Using subtext to drive a character shows us how the character is feeling without having to say directly what that feeling is or why it is important.

For example, if a high school student is nervous about asking another student to the prom, their dialogue might sound like this:

> JOHN
> Hey! Um, hey, hey Anna . . . ?
> ANNA
> Yeah?
> JOHN
> I was, you know, thinking about, in the cafeteria today –
> ANNA
> Ugh, I know. What was that lunch they were
> serving us? Blah.
> JOHN
> Oh, yeah, sure, blah, I mean, I kind of like over
> cooked, but whatever, you know, they had the prom
> ticket sales table set up?
> ANNA
> Right. The prom. What an ancient ritual. Who needs
> a prom nowadays?

JOHN

Yeah, like, so old. My Mom's age old. Or, even more, Mesozoic, like dinosaur age, roar! And things. But, whatever. I don't know. It could be fun. The prom. Maybe. If, like, friends, go together, like, really good close friends, and get a limo and hold hands, or not hold hands, or whatever.

(*Anna reaches out and takes and holds John's hand.*)

JOHN

Cool, well, I'll drop by and, like, if I have just extra time, stop by the table and buy us tickets.

ANNA

Cool.

JOHN

Cool.

As an audience member, we can see that John is working up the courage to ask Anna to the prom by the way he speaks – it's more compelling to watch him struggle with asking her than if he simply asks her directly at the beginning of the scene. This choice also suggests the power dynamic in the relationship which might affect future conflicts and actions.

Writing Exercise

Use the following elements to write a short scene full of subtext:

- Characters: A couple in love.
- Situation: One person wants to say "I love you" to the other but is afraid to do so and be rejected.

- Think about: What did writing with subtext do to your characters and their situation? Did it make it more tense, less tense, funnier, sadder? Again, there's no right answer. We just want to explore how you can use subtext as a dramatic tool.

Playwrights think about how they can use subtext to make a moment more powerful onstage.

Overview

Subtext is the hidden conversation underneath the conversation the two characters are having, but, for some reason, the character cannot say it directly. Since we are writing for performance, using subtext is especially potent because the audience sees the subtextual struggle (the emotions beneath the words) play out in front of them.

Dialogue and Stage Directions

Dialogue and stage directions work together to bring your play to life on the page. Let's take a look at the second half of the scene between John and Anna:

ANNA
Right. The prom. What an ancient ritual. Who needs a prom nowadays?
JOHN
Yeah, like, so old. My Mom's age old. Or, even more, Mesozoic, like dinosaur age, roar! And

things. But, whatever. I don't know. It could be fun. The prom. Maybe. If, like, friends, go together, like, really good close friends, and get a limo and hold hands, or not hold hands, or whatever.

(Anna reaches out and takes and holds John's hand.)

JOHN

Cool, well, I'll drop by and, like, if I have just extra time, stop by the table and buy us tickets.

Anna says "yes" to John's invitation to go to the prom by simply taking his hand. It's clean and clear and shows her answer (rather than telling it).

Plus, when Anna takes John's hand, everyone in the audience viscerally connects with that moment – there is a moment of palpable emotion in the audience because everyone has had at least one moment where they want to be seen and accepted by someone else. By Anna taking John's hand, we are viscerally connected to that one moment both onstage and within ourselves. The specific moment becomes universal.

Overview

Dialogue and stage directions combine to create powerful moments in a theatrical way.

Collaboration

Typically, only the playwright can change the dialogue. The dialogue is sacrosanct. However, the director can change the stage directions. So, the play might look differently on the stage than the playwright imagines it on the page.

There is a temptation for playwrights to overwrite dialogue in a prescriptive manner to force directors to stage the play exactly as the playwright sees it. I understand this temptation but I encourage you to reflect deeply before making the choice to over write. One of the core elements of making theatre is collaboration. We create more compelling work together.

Does that mean you agree to all of the director's ideas? Of course not. But listen to them, think about whether or not they are a stronger choice for the piece. Don't let your ego keep you from embracing a more interesting choice just because it is not your idea.

Overview

In most communities, only the playwright can change dialogue. However, stage directions might be changed by the director.

Writing Exercise

Use the following prompt to write a scene that combines dialogue and stage directions to create a moment of theatre.

Write a short scene between two best friends. One best friend is trying to tell the other best friend that she is moving far away from her job.

Use one or more of these actions in stage directions to tell the story of the moment in your scene:

- One friend kicks the other.
- One friend hugs the other.
- One friend pushes the other friend out a window.
- One friend gets down on one knee to propose marriage.
- One friend throws a lamp at the other friend.

Think about: Did thinking in physical movement change how you crafted the scene? Did the movement take the place of some dialogue, or did the movement dictate that more dialogue needed to be spoken? Again, there's no right answer. We just want to explore how you can use dialogue and stage directions together as a dramatic tool.

Playwrights combine dialogue and stage directions to make a moment more powerful onstage.

Resources
Student Favorites

The plays listed here were some of my students' favorites for illustrating the lessons in this chapter.

- *Utility* by Emily Schwend (Yale Press)
  - Amber struggles to work two jobs and raise a family alongside on-again, off-again charming husband Chris in East Texas. Told with minimal stage directions.

- *An Ideal Husband* by Oscar Wilde (Project Gutenberg/eBook #885)
  - This witty 19th-century comedy of blackmail and political corruption. Told with stage directions throughout.

Additional Resource

- Playwrights on stagecraft: youtu.be/IFDZzbWG fKI?si=HyNVEEgq9FV5TBfS (National Theatre/ London)

Discussed in Chapter

- *Bottle Fly* by Jacqueline Goldfinger (Yale Press)
- *Detroit '67* by Dominique Morriseau (Oberon Modern Plays)
- *Miss Julie* by August Strindberg (translated by Edwin Björkman, *Miss Julia*/Project Gutenberg/ eBook #14347)

Notes

1 It is important to note that Morisseau used "Everybody Needs Love" in her play. That song is copyrighted material, so she got permission to use the song. If you are using the work of another artist in your own work, then you need their permission unless their work is in the public domain. Learn more about copyright in the U.S. here: copyright.gov/what-is-copyright/

2 Printed with permission of playwright, 2024.

8

Exposition

Exposition is information about a character and their world. Part of the work of a playwright is figuring out what exposition needs to be shared, and what does not.

Exposition

As we saw in the Christmas example in the last chapter, when we're learning about our characters, the first dialogue that occurs to us is often expository. Expository means that you simply state the obvious information needed to understand your characters in that moment.

> CHARACTER
> I hate my mother, and that's why I'm not going to Christmas.

However, as you write, think about how you can turn this exposition into active scene work.

For example, by the end of the Christmas scene revision, we'd come to:

> *The main character slams down the phone, throws the carefully prepared turkey into the garbage, and grabs take-out menus.*

DOI: 10.4324/9781003505310-10

CHARACTER
Someone must be delivering on Christmas.
CHARACTER'S ROOMMATE
How's your Mom?
CHARACTER
The place on Park Street delivers. I'll get you a #33.

The exposition – the Character has chosen no to attend Christmas dinner, and instead, she's staying home and ordering take-out with her roommate – is shown through action.

This is an example of moving from an expository moment to an active moment that includes exposition.

Here is an example of an active moment that includes exposition in an engaging way from playwright Fatima Dike's play *So What's New?*

Mercedes, a teenage girl, returns home from sports practice in the evening. Dee, her mother, thinks that staying out late after school will lead to trouble. This scene could easily lead to a long passage of unwieldly exposition. However, Dike chooses to dramatize a specific moment of conflict that exemplifies the mother-daughter dispute. At the beginning of the scene, Mercedes enters with her school bag.

MERCEDES Ma, what's cooking I'm starving?
DEE Mercedes, what time is it?
MERCEDES Has your watch stopped, Ma?
DEE I asked you a question? Lixesha lokungena endlini eli? [This is no time for a girl to be out on the street.]

MERCEDES Hayi.

DEE Uyabonake mtwanam [Listen here my child]. In
this house, we have rules. If you feel you can't obey
them, move out.

MERCEDES But Ma, today is Wednesday. We have
netball practice.

DEE Netball practice my foot, Mercedes! If netball
is going to keep you out this late, you'll have to
give it up.

MERCEDES Give it up?

DEE Yes.

MERCEDES But Ma, I've been picked to play in the
first team.

DEE Today your excuse is netball practice, tomorrow
it will still be netball practice. You are still a baby.
I don't want you dropping another baby on my
lap. Your father died mtwanami, without leaving
us a cent. I want you to learn and make your own
future. I want you to bring me a degree, not a birth
certificate, siyavana?[1]

At the beginning of the scene, we jump into an
immediate conflict about coming home late. Dike
waits until the end of the scene to reveal the mother's
underlying concern about her daughter getting preg-
nant. This way, Dike immediately grabs our attention
and then builds to a big reveal. Dike makes this
moment about more than coming home late; she
makes it about preserving Mercedes's potential to live
a better life.

Writing Exercise

Write out a favorite family story in paragraph form.

Write out a section of that story in dialogue and stage directions.

Now, select one to three moments where you could have a character(s) show the moment in some way or create a moment of conflict rather than simply telling information.

Revise those moments to be more active.

What did you keep in? What did you leave out? What did you change? This is the type of revision that playwrights engage in on a regular basis.

Another way that playwrights activate exposition is to bring two characters into conflict over a choice that one character must make *right now*.

For example, in this short exchange from playwright Carlo Goldoni's *A Curious Mishap* (18th century), the servant Gascoigne is packing his master's [boss's] trunk for a long trip when Marianna, his love interest, enters.

Through the action of Marianna trying to convince Gascoigne not to go on the trip with his boss, we learn important exposition about Gascoigne, his boss, and their trip. Goldoni's exposition also shows the action of the scene in two ways:

- First, it shows the action is by having two characters in direct opposition to one another; they each want different things, and they cannot both get what they want (i.e., Gascoigne wants to go, but Marianna wants him to stay – so someone is going to lose this argument).
- Second, Gascoigne is literally packing luggage for the trip; by physically continuing to pack the bag onstage – rather than stopping packing when Marianna asks him to stay – we receive a visual cue that he is still going on the trip, regardless of what she says.

The exposition is activated through both physical and verbal conflict.

[*Gascoigne, packing his master's trunk. Enter Marianna.*]

Marianna. May I wish good-morning to Monsieur Gascoigne?

Gascoigne. Yes, my sweet Marianna, I thank you for your good-morning, but good-night would be more agreeable to me from your lips.

Marianna. [*sees him packing the trunk*] From what I see, I should rather wish you a pleasant journey.

Gascoigne. Oh, my precious jewel, such a melancholy departure must be followed by a most doleful journey!

Marianna. Then you are sorry to go?

Gascoigne. How can you doubt it? After having enjoyed
   your delightful society for six months, can I leave
   you without the deepest sorrow?

Marianna. And who forces you to do what is so
   disagreeable?

Gascoigne. [*keeps packing*] Do you not know?
   My master.

Marianna. Masters are not wanting at the Hague, and
   you can easily find one who will give you better
   wages than a poor French officer.

Gascoigne. Pardon me, such language does not become so
   good a girl as you are. I have for many years had the
   honour of serving my excellent master. I have attended
   him in the war, and have not shunned danger to show
   my fidelity. He is poor, but never man had a better
   heart. Were he promoted, I am sure I should share his
   good fortune. Would you desire me to abandon him,
   and let him return to France without me?

Marianna. You speak like the worthy fellow you are;
   but I cannot conceal my affection for you.

Gascoigne. Dear Marianna, I am as much distressed as
   you are, but I hope to see you again, and then to be
   able to say, Here I am, I can support you, and, if
   you wish it, I am yours.

Marianna. Heaven grant it!

The exposition is activated by conflict over a choice that
must be made right now.

Another way playwrights activate exposition is by
introducing a character who is new to the situation, so

the character must have the situation explained to them. This introduction of a new character and short exposition leads to an action.

For example, in a contemporary scene from the story paper of *Nonomiya/The Shrine in the Field*[2] (14th century), we see how introducing a new character can help activate exposition and lead to action:

- In the scene, there is a Village Woman at the Shrine, and the Monk asks the Village Woman to tell the story of the mysterious Lady Rokujō because he wants to know what happened to her.
- The Village Woman tells the story of Lady Rokujō, whose heart was broken by the Shining Prince at this shrine on this day many years ago. The Prince left, and Lady Rokujō was left alone, filled with despair and obsession over her lost love.
- After the Village Woman tells the Monk this story, she implores the Monk to pray for the peace of her soul.
- She exits, and the Monk realizes that the Village Woman is the ghost of Lady Rokujō, who cannot find peace because she is still tormented by obsession.
- This realization leads him to decide to stay nearby and pray for the peace of her soul.

The Village Woman's telling of the story – the exposition – is activated because Lady Rokujō's ghost wants something and goes after it – to tell her story so the Monk will pray for her – and the Monk hears the story (receiving new information) and takes action (based on that new information) – he chooses to pray for her soul.

Here is the scene between the Village Woman and the Monk. (Note that "Reciters" are a chorus of performers who speak together.)

2. The Village Woman Narrates a Story and Disappears

Responding to the request of the Monk, the woman narrates the life of Lady Rokujō then disappears.

Monk	Would you please tell me more about Lady Rokujō?
Reciters	Lady Rokujō was the beloved wife of the previous Crown Prince, who was a younger brother of Emperor Kiritsubo and who fully enjoyed his prosperous life. The relationship between the couple was as sweet as the relationship between a flower and its scent.
Woman	However, following the law of this world that you must separate with those you meet,
Reciters	just as it were a brief dream, she was bereaved of her husband.
Woman	She however could not submerge the rest of her life in tears as a widow.
Reciters	The Shining Prince, Hikaru Genji, assertively started to visit Lady Rokujō in secret.
Woman	No one knows why his heart changed.
Reciters	His visits came to a halt. Even so, Genji did not completely fall out of love with Lady Rokujō. His tender and delicate feelings for

her brought him to visit Lady Rokujō far away at Nonomiya Shrine in Sagano. All the autumn flowers had already withered, and the singing of insects became scarce and weak. On his way to Nonomiya, the wind blew in the pine trees, making the pine branches cry and even increasing his loneliness. Genji's sadness endlessly increased in late autumn. Genji arrived at this Nonomiya Shrine and spoke wholeheartedly sincere words to Lady Rokujō, but he felt sadness in the depths of his heart.

Woman   After parted from Genji, her daughter purified herself in Katsura River on the day she departed to Ise.

Reciters   Floating down branches of *sakaki* tree tied with pieces of white cotton in a river, just as the whiten floating grasses, Lady Rokujō followed the stream of her forlorn heart and left Nonomiya for the Suzuka River. She read a poem to Genji, "Even though I dampen myself in the waves of the Suzuka River with tears, who will remember me, going to Ise, in Kyoto?" It was unprecedented that a mother accompanied a shrine maiden to live at Ise Shrine. She was filled with the deepest remorse for going to Ise with her daughter.

Reciters   Listening to your stories, you do not sound like just a villager. Would you please give me your name?

Woman	It is shameful that my name is known, for I am a menial woman whose name is unworthy to be mentioned. If you really want to know it, please pray for the peace of my soul in another world as a woman without a name.
Reciters	Are you identifying yourself as a deceased woman? How mysterious! You must have had to leave
Woman	this world regretfully. A long, long time has past since then, and only the name is left in the world.
Reciters	The Lady Rokujō is
Woman	myself.
Reciters	Revealing her identity, in the breeze of autumn evening, the lady quietly disappears, hiding behind the two posts of a torii gate standing in dim light in the woods illuminated by the evening moon. The lady quietly disappears as if hiding.[3]

After this scene, the Monk begins to pray to console the soul of the Lady. This scene is an example of introducing a new character to activate exposition and lead to action.

Writing Exercise

Look at the moments you wrote in the last writing exercise.

Add a character who enters the moment and does not know what's going on – how does this change how you activate exposition?

Activating exposition is key to the success of your play. As you evolve as a writer, you'll learn how to better work with expository moments.

Overview

Exposition is the straightforward sharing of information. Playwrights activate exposition.

Object Work

Playwrights use objects to show their characters' internal emotions as well. You can imbue objects with layers of meaning which help you externalize the story.

In the Christmas example in the last chapter, I use the turkey to shows us that there has been a change within the character. Let's break that down:

- In the beginning, the character has carefully prepared the turkey for her family's Christmas party. The turkey symbolizes special occasions and family.
- Now, the turkey is thrown into the trash can. The character's relationship to the turkey has changed – but the turkey is just a symbol of her family and a special occasion. So, we understand that it's actually the relationship to her family and/or the special occasion that has changed.
- Next, she embraces take-out food – the food of the ordinary and everyday. We see that the anger expressed through throwing away the turkey

manifests itself in her changing her plans. She had completely done away with her family and the holiday, and reverts to the business of everyday life.

The audience may not consciously break down the use of the turkey into smaller actions but they understand the feelings behind the use of that object immediately. In a 10-second interaction, we have given them a significant amount of information about the story and characters.

In early drafts, even the writer might not be able to break down their own plays with this much specificity. But, as they move through subsequent drafts, they pay attention to every detail.

Writing Exercise

Grab the object closest to you. (For example, a gold-plated pen.)

Brainstorm four to six types of people who might have that object and what they might use it for. (For example, a student might use a pen to put her hair in a bun while studying. Or, a boss might break a pen in half.)

Pick one person and situation. Now, free write a narrative paragraph(s) of what meaning that object could hold. (For example, the boss throwing the pen. That pen might have been used to sign an important document that was going to save the company from financial disaster. The boss thought the deed was done, and they'd saved their company. But they've just learned that an employee made a mistake that put the company in financial jeopardy again, immediately, today. In anger, the boss breaks the pen in half, which expresses his anger about the failure to save his business in an active and visual way for the stage.)

Now, sketch out a quick dialogue and stage directions that show this scene.

Playwrights write a first draft, then step back and look at the draft. They think about what objects can be used in new and interesting ways to show the character's feelings about a situation.

Overview

We use objects to externalize a character's internal experience.

Plant and Payoff

One popular way to externalize a character's internal journey is to "plant" and "payoff" objects or language.

For example, let's say a woman's mother dies, and the woman falls into a deep despair. The woman is given her mother's prized heart-shaped locket. Emotionally, she is in a place of pain, and physically, we see that she cannot wear the locket; it is too emotionally painful for her to put it physically around her neck. Instead, she puts the locket away in a drawer where she will not be able to see it. The playwright has "planted" the idea that this locket is imbued with the pain of her mother's death.

Then, throughout the play, as the woman begins to heal emotionally, she can look at the locket without sobbing. Then, she can hold the locket lovingly. Finally, she can wear the locket around her neck. Being able to wear the locket signifies that the woman has found a place of emotional healing; she can wear her mother's locket in joy instead of in pain. The locket is now a fond remembrance. The locket has now "paid off" because it has shown the character's journey.

Overview

"Plant" and "Payoff" mean repeatedly using objects or language in new ways to externalize the internal life of a character and add meaning to the play.

Writing Exercise

Look at the moments you wrote in the last writing exercise.

Take one of the moments that you dramatized and add an object that holds meaning for a character. Is there a way that you can use that object to show some of the character's emotions? For example, if the character is made at their best friend's, perhaps they take the best friend's picture and tear it up rather than simply yelling at the friend.

Playwrights continually ask themselves, "How can I externalize this onstage?"

Check-In

If you are using this book to write a full play, before moving on to the next chapter, make sure that you have at least one protagonist and one antagonist for your new play. Make a list of ways they might be in opposition to one another. Select at least one of these oppositions that you are interested in exploring in your first draft. Use some of the writing exercises within the chapter to begin discovering their voices.

Resources

Student Favorites

The plays listed here were some of my students' favorites for illustrating the lessons in this chapter.

- Kushner, Tony, *Angels in America, Part One: Millenium Approaches* (Theatre Communications Group)
  - A complex, often metaphorical, and at times symbolic examination of AIDS and homosexuality in the United States in the 1980s.
- *Flyin' West* by Pearl Cleage (*Flyin' West and Other Plays*/Theatre Communications Group)
  - Straight-forward narrative about pioneers who settled the all-Black town of Nicodemus, Kansas, face problems ranging from the inevitability of long, cold winters to continued racial strife, protect themselves and one another with humor, love, hope, and resilience.

- *New Dramaturgies: Strategies and Exercises for 21st Century Playwriting* by Mark Bly. For exposition, focus on "Bly's *Einstein's Dreams* Exercise." (Routledge 2021)

Discussed in Chapter

- *410 [Gone]* by Frances Ya-Chu Cowhig (Dramatist Play Service)
- *A Curious Mishap* by Carlo Goldoni (edited by Helen Zimmern/Project Gutenberg/eBook #33575)
- *Nonomiya/The Shrine in the Field* story paper by www.the-noh.com/
- *So What's New* by Fatima Dike (*South African Women Playwrights*/Routledge)

Notes

1 "So What's New?" by Fatima Dike, *Black South African Women: An Anthology of Plays*, edited by Kathy A. Perkins, Copyright 1998 by Routledge.
2 Text data: provided by the-noh.com (https://www.the-noh.com/).
3 Full English language scripts are available at: the-noh.com

9
Story and Plot

Story* and plot* comprise what your audience sees onstage (plot) and what they understand happens both onstage and off (story).

Story and Plot

The story is the big picture of your play. The story encompasses both what we see onstage and what we think happens offstage. The story includes what happens before the play begins, what happens during the play, and what we think happens after the play ends.

The plot is only what we see happen onstage.

For example, in *Cinderella*, we see the stepmother order Cinderella to scrub the floor. The stepmother is part of the plot. But we also know that Cinderella had a biological mother who died and whom we never see. Both the stepmother and the mother are part of the story.

Writing Exercise and Optional Group Exercise

Pick a fairytale or myth. Pick your favorite version of that myth. Or, if you are in a group, have one person in that group tell the story of that fairytale or myth.

 DOI: 10.4324/9781003505310-11

Think about, or discuss as a group, what moments in that story might make interesting plot points to see onstage as part of the storytelling.

Now, what might not be interesting to see, but is part of the story, so we need to know it in order to understand what we see onstage?

Make a list of what could be part of your story and a separate list of what could be a part of your plot.

Separating what is in your plot (what happens onstage) versus what is in your story (what happens offstage and on) is one way of helping you think about your play. This is especially useful in the revision process when you're refining your play.

During the pre-writing process, some writers chose to write out the story in narrative form (like a short story) in as much detail as they can imagine.

For example, if they are writing *Cinderella*, they write out the details of the mother's death, how Cinderella reacted at the time, and what happened afterward. This gives the writer a deeper understanding of the character, even if the audience will not see these moments onstage.

Other playwrights chose to outline the plot in advance – writing down what they think will happen onstage to tell this story; for example, we see Cinderella fight with her stepmother about the ball.

Even other playwrights chose not to differentiate between story and plot when they begin writing.

Instead, they write moments or scenes or movements or dialogue that speak to them. This helps them get the words on the page to begin a play.

There are many ways to approach the writing process. As you learn more about yourself and your playwright-brain, you'll discover what process works for you. What's important to remember is that the audience will:

- Witness what occurs onstage (plot and story).
- Make assumptions about what occurs offstage (story).

They will combine information about the plot and story to draw conclusions about your characters and what the play means.

Writing Exercise

Pick a favorite play or movie.

Write a short narrative description of the story in paragraph form.

Make a list of the plot points you see portrayed onstage or on screen.

Reflect on the differences between what you see literally happen onstage or on screen (the plot) and what you know happened overall in the fleshed-out story.

When you're writing, and especially when you're revising, you'll decide how much plot is necessary to communicate the overall story. Frequently, playwrights add/subtract plot pieces as they write and revise.

Overview

The story is the big picture of your play, and the plot is what is seen onstage.

Present Tense-ness

Theatrical plots are written in the present tense. The characters are living their experience in their present moment. You might write a play that takes place in another time period. But we write from an active present – whenever that "present moment" is in which our characters are living.

As we saw in the scene from Dike's *So What's New?* in the last chapter, the action is taking place *right now* both onstage and in the story:

MERCEDES Ma, what's cooking I'm starving?

DEE Mercedes, what time is it?

MERCEDES Has your watch stopped, Ma?

DEE I asked you a question? Lixesha lokungena endlini eli? [This is no time for a girl to be out on the street.]

MERCEDES Hayi.

DEE Uyabonake mtwanam [Listen here my child]. In this house, we have rules. If you feel you can't obey them, move out.

MERCEDES But Ma, today is Wednesday. We have netball practice.

In this excerpt, actions are occurring *right now:* Mercedes's practice just ended, Dee has been waiting for her, and Mercedes walks through the door and directly into a conflict with her mother – it is all happening in the present tense.

This is one reason plays feel relevant and resonate because we are experiencing them alongside the characters who are living them in the same moment. There is a special power in experiencing something with another human being – in this case, with an actor onstage as a character living a brand new moment with you.

Theatre is about Here/Us/Now from playwright Michael Hollinger[1] of Sing the Body Electric:

Theatre is all about "Here/Now/Us" – these characters, in this place, right now – not "There/Them/Them" – other people, in some other place, at another time. That's why stage directions are always in present tense: Maggie takes a swig, instead of Maggie took a swig. Of course, we can set plays in faraway times and places (e.g., 13th-century France, or 19th-century London, or 1950s Boston, or St. Louis, MO, on December 7, 1941), but it's always here-and-now for the characters. So it's our job as playwrights to generate as much "present-tenseness" as possible.

If one character tells another a story about the time her father nearly drowned in 7th grade, that's pretty much the definition of There/Then/Them: relating something that happened to somebody else at another place and time. If she tells the story about her own near-drowning, we get a little more present; if she tells it as she's revisiting the pool for the first time, a little

---

more. If the incident is actually re-enacted (even if the stage is completely dry), it's Here/Now/Us, about as immediate as you can get.

Naturally, there are moments in plays where characters relate past experiences – all good, and a daily occurrence in real life. The task then is to figure out how the telling itself – this character conveying this story in this place and time – is a present-tense event. Is she telling the story to warn? To threaten? To gain sympathy? To divulge a long-held secret? To seduce? In general, the more Here/Now/Us, the better.

Overview

Plays are written in the present tense. The characters are experiencing the moments of the plot as if they are happening to them at that moment.

Resources
Student Favorites

The plays listed here were some of my students' favorites for illustrating the lessons in this chapter.

- *Blood Wedding* by Frederico García Lorca (*Three Plays*/Farrar, Straus and Giroux)
  - A tragic love story about a couple that rebels against the constraints of society, run away together, and face an uncertain future. This play is told in chronological order.

- *Stop Kiss* by Diana Son (Overlook Press)
  - Sara and Callie endure a vicious homophobic attack which transforms their lives in ways they never imagined. This play is told out of chronological order.

Additional Resource

- *Ghost Light: An Introductory Handbook for Dramaturgy* by Michael Mark Chemers offers a beginner's guide to dramaturgy. For now, focus on *Part Two: Analysis.* (Southern Illinois University Press 2010)

Discussed in Chapter

- *Cinderella* (Disney film, 1950)
- *Sing the Body Electric* by Micheal Hollinger (Theatrical Rights Worldwide/TRW Plays)
- *So What's New* by Fatima Dike (*South African Women Playwrights*/Routledge)

Note

1 Printed with permission of playwright, 2024.

10
Play World

The world of your play is the world in which your characters live. The play world can look similar to your own or very, very different. When we create a play world, we get to decide how it looks, works, smells, and feels. It's a fully immersive experience.

Play World

The play world is the world your characters inhabit. This does not have to be the literal earth; instead, it's wherever, whenever, and however your characters are experiencing their world – a world that only exists in your play.

Your play world influences how your characters behave and, therefore, influences other elements of your play like action and conflict.

For example, in Little Red Riding Hood's world, the woods are cold and scary, the Wolf is in disguise, and the Grandmother's House is a place of brightness, warmth, and love. Little Red only accepts help from the Wolf because he's disguised as a kind, gentle Billy Goat. The woods are terrifying, so she is happy to ride on the Billy Goat through the woods to be safe. She never would have accepted help from a stranger and showed him where Grandma lives if (a) she knew he was a wolf and (b) the woods were not too frightening to navigate on her own. The author designs a play world that forces Little Red to make active choices that change the course of the story.

Nothing happens by accident in our play world. Everything is a choice made for a reason.

In early drafts, playwrights sometimes over-write or describe their play worlds to learn more about them and understand how they function. Then, later in the process, playwrights edit down and sculpt their play worlds to be more specific.

In addition, the world of your play can change if that choice supports what you are trying to do with your play.

For example, playwright Luigi Pirandello's comedy *Six Characters in Search of an Author* begins with a realistic moment of an acting company preparing to rehearse a play. In the middle of rehearsal, they are interrupted by the arrival of six strangers who are the unfinished characters from the play in search of the author who can finish writing their story.

The entrance* of these strangers signals to us that there is a change in the world of the play. We thought we were watching a realistic play but we are now in an absurd world where imaginary characters come to life. This breaking of strict reality to create a new play world is joyful and fun. It allows Pirandello to take the story in a new direction by redefining the characteristics of the play world. However, once the shift is made in the play world – the characters and story conform to the rules of the new play world, the rules of the realistic world are left behind.

By the time the strangers exit*, we've seen an entirely different story than we expected to see at the beginning of the play.

Regardless of whether your play world stays the same all the way through or shifts in some way, it is always the world your characters live within.

Your play world is also an extension of the "here and now" of your characters. It is how their world actively functions at their moment in time.

In her popular essay, *Visit to a Small Planet*, Elinor Fuchs writes:

> A play is not a flat work of literature, not a description in poetry of another world, but is in itself another world passing before you in time and space. Language is only one part of this world . . . To see this entire world, do this literally: Mold the play into a medium-sized ball, set it before you in the middle distance, and squint your eyes. Make the ball small enough that you can see the entire planet, not so small that you lose detail, and not so large that detail overwhelms the whole . . . Before you is the "world of the play."[1]

I swear by the essay "Visit to a Small Planet" by Elinor Fuchs.

(MIT's free, public version: https://web.mit.edu/ jscheib/Public/foundations_06/ef_smallplanet.pdf)

It reminds me to never assume that there's any one form that a play (or any other piece of art) should take. It reminds me that theatrical norms are just norms (not universal truths), and were largely created by folks whose perspectives, politics, & experiences differ from mine. It invites me to question the givens (like naturalism*, linearity, likeable characters, a protagonist, a traditional play arc, etc.), and it emboldens me to be radically open to learning THIS playworld – its style & shape, its voice & values.

One of my favorite things to do when I'm partway through a first draft – or about to start a rewrite – is to step back and take stock of the playworld itself. If helpful, here are some prompts I love for expanding, enriching, or revising my new play:

i. This play (or world) sounds like . . .
ii. This play/world moves like . . .
iii. This play/world feels like . . .
iv. This play/world looks like . . .
v. This play/world smells & tastes like . . .
vi. Time in this play/word . . .
vii. Space in this play/world . . .

viii. Characters in this play/world . . .
ix. Power in this play/world . . .
x. Language in this play/world . . .
xi. The human body in this play/world . . .
xii. Describe (or draw) the shape of this play.
xiii. What is the absolute opposite of this play?
xiv. If this play were to shatter into a hundred pieces, what would be in every piece?
xv. What does this play seem to be asking, begging, or demanding that you do? (What is it needing from you?)

Your Fellow Writer,

L M Feldman[2]

Thrive, Or What You Will [An Epic]

As you write, stop and take time to investigate the world of the play. Close your eyes. Imagine walking its streets. Attend its schools. Lurk in its alleyways.

Here are a few questions to ask yourself about your play world to get you started:

- Think about your world geographically: Are there tall buildings? Vast prairies? What is space like on your planet? What is the climate in the world of your play? Is the sun always shining warmly or burning through their skin?
- Think about your world spiritually: Is there a primary religion or spiritual belief system? Are there many? Is your character a part of one or any of them? How does spirituality shape the way the world works?

- Think about your world socially: Are there class rules? Aristocracy? Who has power on this planet? How is power achieved and maintained?
- Think about the mood of your world: Is it generally happy? Sad? Ironic? (The mood will be connected to the tone of your play. We'll discuss tone later in the book.)

Writing Exercise

Go sit in a park or playground. Begin by answering the questions that Feldman posed previously then expand on your answers. You do not need to remain entirely realistic – there could be things in the world that denote non-realistic realms.

Now, think of a character who belongs in this play world. Write a monologue where they are walking through the park. What do they see? Feel? What do the children playing on the seesaw mean to them?

Practicing building play worlds is a fun and useful way to begin thinking more holistically about the world your characters inhabit.

Playwrights use elements of design to illuminate their play worlds. Some popular elements of design used to represent play worlds include music, movement, repetition, costume, set, prop, lighting effects, and sound effects.

For example, in playwright Jordan Harrison's *Kid Simple: A radio play in the flesh,* Moll, a girl who invents things, wins the science fair with a machine for hearing sounds that can't be heard. She goes on a wild adventure that requires the use of this special invention for her – and the audience – to hear unique sounds that shapes the journey of the play. Often, these unique sounds are created live on stage by a foley artist. The inclusion of foley sound externalizes and symbolizes her magical machine.

Play words can also influence dialogue.

For example, in Idris Goodwin's *How We Got On*, Hank, Julian, and Luann are three talented, determined suburban teens coming of age in the 1980s. They dream of fame and fortune in the new Hip-Hop music scene, and so their dialogue is peppered with rhythms and rhymes influenced by Hip-Hop music. This gives the world a feel of movement, rhythm, and tight pacing that keeps us engaged with the world of the play.

Fun Fact

Revolving Stages: Revolving stages (stages that move in a circle or have sections that revolve) were invented by playwright Nakimi Shōzō of *The Feathery Garment from Heaven* to help move heavy seats more quickly so that scene changes could be quicker and smoother. This invention helped playwrights and their collabora-tors* control the pacing of the show and revolutionized the theatre.

The play world is different from the setting. The play world is the full universe your characters inhabit. The setting is what we see onstage.

For example, in *Kid Simple,* Moll's sound machine is entirely real in her play world. However, this magical machine would not literally work in our real world on a stage. So, producers to use a foley artist to bring sound into the room. The foley artist and their instruments theatrically represent what Moll's machine would sound like in her play world.

The play world is the world of the characters. The setting is the short description of what you think you need onstage to represent your play world.

Overview

Nothing happens by accident in our play world. Everything is a choice made for a reason.

Rules of the World

Your play world has its own rules. By rules, I mean there's an internal logic to how the world functions.

For example, in a superhero movie, someone with special powers will save the day. That's a rule of those worlds. Or, if a play is set in the 1400s with strict attention to period detail, then you're not going to see the characters use machine guns. The constraints of the time period are a rule of the world.

By respecting the rules of your world, you create a more dynamic story that an audience can follow.

For example, in playwright Alice Childress's *Trouble in Mind*, she sets her play in the realistic world of a rehearsal room where artists are rehearsing a play. The play asks questions about how art can uphold racist stereotypes* even as the artists attempt to avoid them. Since the play world is a theatre space – and the audience is seated in an actual theatre space when watching the play – there is a direct connection made between the theater-makers on stage and their audience. Childress uses her play world to point out that these aren't just questions in a made-up play world; these are questions that pertain to you and how you engage with art right now, in this moment, as you sit there, and watch this play.

Your characters might also live in two different play worlds at the same time.

For example, in playwright Alice Gerstenberg's adaptation of *Alice's Adventures in Wonderland,* we see that there are two different worlds – everyday life and life on the other side of the looking glass (a large mirror).

When the character is in the play world of everyday life we know what to expect; cats meow and games like chess are played normally. But when she goes through the looking glass the play world changes; animals talk, characters speak in riddles, and nature loops and shifts unrealistically. By knowing the "rules" of these two worlds we engage in the fun of traveling within and between both worlds – but we also have enough context for each world in order to understand what is going on within them.

Sometimes, you create rules of the world, and then you break those rules at an important moment to emphasize that moment, plot point, idea, or other element of the play. This break ends one play world and begins another one. The characters now live by the rules of the brand new play world. For that "break" in the rules to be effective, you need a clear world with clear rules to "break" so the audience can track when the "break" occurs.

For example, in Pirandello's *Six Characters . . .,* the break in the play is clear and significant; we have been holding a realistic rehearsal, and now six unfinished characters enter, the realistic world is broken, and now the play shifts into a more absurdly comic world.

The "break" gives Pirandello the freedom to move into a new realm, but it also creates new rules for his play world that he must live inside of for the audience to be able to understand what is happening onstage.

Overview

As you write and revise, you set the rules of your play world and adhere to that logic. Sometimes, the rules of your play world unfurl in the first draft; sometimes, it takes multiple drafts to understand how to define the rules of your play world.

Use of Time as a Creative Element

Time is a malleable creative element of your play.

On stage, how time functions depends upon the needs of the play. Perhaps a day lasts 24 hours – and you are approximating real life – or perhaps a day lasts four months – and you are elongating time. Years can pass in a single scene or between scenes, or you can have a play occur in real time.

In addition to how time works in your larger play world, you can play with time in individual moments to amplify the impact of those moments.

For example, in Shakespeare's *Romeo & Juliet,* the moment that the lovers meet, their immediate attraction stops the world. Everything around them fades into the distance as they speak and move in ways that show how they are feeling inside. A moment that would take 30 seconds in everyday time takes a few minutes in stage time. By elongating and highlighting that moment of electric connection, the audience understands more deeply the power of that connection – a connection so powerful that the lovers will do anything to maintain it.

Time can also speed up a series of moments.

For example, in playwright Jennifer Haley's futuristic *The Nether,* the plot revolves around a Detective investigating a crime that happens in an online world. Haley writes short scenes with sharp dialogue. She condenses time into short spurts, which gives the play world the feel of a jagged rollercoaster ride that might run off the rails. This choice highlights the relationship between reality and online, one that overlaps, ebbs, and crashes into one another, leading to dangerous outcomes.

In plays, time can leap years and centuries in a moment. Time can move forward or backward or stop moving at all.

In addition to considering how time works within the script, be aware that time works differently for the audience in their experience as well. Unlike books or streaming a movie, we can't flip back a few pages or rewind. We experience an individual moment uniquely and only once (as we do in life), which makes theatre a particularly temporal form of storytelling.

Overview

You can use time in many ways in your plays, both as a function of the world and also as a function of individual moments and scenes.

Thoughts on where a play lives from playwright Caridad Svich of Red Bike:

Where does a play live? What is its place? Location is sometimes described as the setting of a play but setting and place are not the same thing!

The place is where the story of the play is located (in Illyria, Boston, the netherworld, etc.) [EDITORIAL INSERT: "The place" meaning the Play World.]

The setting is what we see and experience on stage.

When you write a play, think about the setting far more than the place or places, even though they inform one another. And if your play is situated on stage, you still need to think about what the visual experience of that setting is! Remember that even the "empty stage" is not empty! So, imagine the setting. As if you were walking into a gallery or museum. What do we see? What does it feel like? What are the textures and materials of the setting? Wood, glass, plastic, fabric? What are the central elements you can see?

As a playwright, you are looking for a central image that distills the experience of the play in visual/textural terms. Even when the front matter of a play doesn't tell you what the setting is, it often can be imagined by what the play-text itself evokes! Yes, words are images in theater and vice versa. Think visually even when you are writing dialogue. Words are action-images. Think like a poet! Because poetry and playwriting are twins.[3]

Check-In

If writing a play as you move through this book, then make sure you've begun brainstorming their play world. At the very least, have a sense of how it looks (their private space, public spaces they inhabit) and their favorite and least favorite places within it.

Resources
Student Favorites

The plays listed here were some of my students' favorites for illustrating the lessons in this chapter.

- *Arlington* by Enda Walsh (Nick Hern Books)
  - A dystopian drama that is poetic and movement-driven, so the play world is built with a wide array of theatrical tools outside of dialogue.

- *The Lieutenant of Inishmore* by Martin McDonagh (Metheun)
  - A farcical look at political violence during the Troubles in Northern Ireland in which a mutilated cat sets off a murderous cycle of revenge.

- *Raisin in the Sun* by Lorraine Hansberry (Vintage)
  - The story of a Black family's experiences in south Chicago as they attempt to improve their financial circumstances with an insurance payout following the death of their father.

Additional Resource

- *Bird By Bird: Some Instructions on Writing and Life* is a book by Anne Lamott for fiction writers; however, it contains good advice for all writers. Focus on the section *The Writing Frame of Mind.* (Anchor, 2007)

Notes

1 *Visit to a Small Planet* by Elinor Fuchs, https://web.mit.edu/jscheib/Public/foundations_06/ef_smallplanet.pdf
2 Printed with permission of playwright, 2024.
3 Printed with permission of playwright, 2024.

11
Theme and Idea

The theme(s) of your play are the underlying ideas that you're exploring.

Theme and Idea

The themes of your play are ideas that you repeat and highlight throughout the play that connect with the state of the world outside the play – the real world your audience lives in.

These concerns can be social and political as well as personal and intimate. You can speak directly to these concerns, or you can layer them in as subtext* and allow the audience to draw their own conclusions.

The theme(s) of your play depend on how you write your play.

For example, you could rewrite the folktale "Cinderella" in many ways. The way that you write the play will determine the theme. You could:

- Write a version in which Cinderella feels that she's being treated like a child instead of a young woman. The theme of that version could be the importance

    DOI: 10.4324/9781003505310-13

of coming-of-age and taking adult responsibility for your life.

- Write a version where Cinderella wants to go to the ball but chooses not to because she wants to obey her Stepmother's rules. The theme of that version could be the importance of following your parents' rules.
- Write a version where Cinderella likes the Prince and leaves with him to escape her horrible family but doesn't really love him. The theme of that version could be how far people will go to escape oppressive situations.

How you choose to write the play affects the themes you highlight in your play.

Some playwrights have a theme in mind early in their writing process; others do not.

For example, playwright Tyrfingur Tyrfingsson of *The Beauty Show* entered his process with a theme in mind:

> As a gay kid, I obsessed over the self-proclaimed founding father of the Scandinavian beauty queen, Mr. Heidar Jonsson.

> Heidar conquered the world of glamour. He took on the roles of a beautician for Yves Saint Laurent, a beauty pageant trainer, and a color analyst. But in the late 90s, at a party, a young man secretly recorded Heidar exhibiting his peculiar perversions. The first video in Iceland to go viral. Heidar was cancelled. He lost everything. He fled the country.

The only reason Heidar survived the guilt and the humiliation, was his faith in beauty. To this day, it sustains him. And that's what *The Beauty Show* is about – a belief in beauty that first destroys your life, but then might just save it.

While Tyrfingsson began with this general idea, he did not write a biographical play about Heidar (although he could have, and that would have been a valid choice). Instead, he writes a play set on Christmas Eve. The urbane couple Luna and Ingi are sitting at home but would prefer to be somewhere else. When there is a knock on the door, we expect it to be a Christmas-type character (Santa Claus? Father Christmas?). But, no, it's Heidar, the beautician! Through the character's specific and heightened relationships, we explore the playwright's interest in how beauty both creates and destroys.[1]

Writers who begin with a theme ask questions like:

- My play is about _____.
- My characters care about this because _____.
- These events in their past made them care about this _____.
- Where/How/When are other characters in opposition _____.

The answers to these questions help you theatricalize a theme; always keep in mind *why* your characters care about the theme and *how* that affects their actions.

Some playwrights do not begin with a theme in mind, but as they write, themes begin to emerge. Throughout the writing process, themes evolve and are refined as the writer learns more about the play.

In addition, as you write your characters, they may begin speaking on their own and surprising you with what they say. What they need to say may be different from what you expected them to say, and that might change your theme.

Whether or not a playwright wants to have theme(s) in their play is irrelevant. As creatures, humans make connections between different experiences. Then, they draw conclusions from those connections. As you move closer to a final draft, consider what themes you'd like the audience to take away from the experience and how clearly you do or don't want to make those themes.

Writing Exercise

Pick an idea or theme that you care about. For example: feeding the homeless, volunteer work, or providing mental health care to everyone.

Now, create a list of people who could be involved in conversations about that theme. Select one character from your list.

Write a monologue that digs down into why the character cares about this issue. Does it have something to do with an intimate experience? With their family? With religion?

If you work from a theme or idea, investigate who is involved in issues surrounding those themes and ideas.

Democratic Resolution of Theme and Idea

Occasionally, playwrights give theatre companies the opportunity to choose how the play resolves (or ends) by offering multiple options for the final scene(s) of the play. Since the final scene(s) in the play often highlight the themes of the play, by giving theatre companies control of selecting their final scene(s), the company shapes the themes they are highlighting for the audience. This is a democratic resolution for the play because the final scene(s) of their production are chosen by the company, not by the playwright.

For example, in playwright Antoinette Nwandu's *Pass Over*, Moses and Kitch are Black men in the U.S. oppressed by racist and classist social structures. They dream of finding their promised land. Nwandu wrote three endings to the play where the men do/do not reach a potential promised land. These scenes are available to producing companies. The companies choose the ending for their production based on where their community – their audiences – are in conversations about race and class in the U.S.

This allows the theatre company to choose what conversation will connect most deeply with their audience – acknowledging the importance of the relationship between artist and audience in the theatre.

Nwandu's initial inspiration for writing *Pass Over* was indeed to respond to current events, specifically the tragic story of Trayvon Martin and resulting trial of George Zimmerman. Then, seven months after the 2016 U.S. presidential election [the election of Donald Trump after Barack Obama finished his Presidential term], *Pass Over* premiered at Chicago's Steppenwolf Theatre. "We were so angry, defeated, and couldn't believe what was going on," remembers Nwandu. She channeled her frustration into her writing, using *Pass Over* to spotlight the systemic racism in America and indict those who were complicit in it.

Nwandu has embraced revising *Pass Over*'s ending to continue to engage with the current events – and audience – when and where a production goes up. When the political landscape shifted as a record number of Americans mobilized for the 2018 U.S. midterm elections, Nwandu evaluated the script for the Off-Broadway premiere at Lincoln Center. "Each time I go back with this play, I ask, 'What's happening in the world? Who's actually going to be in those seats?'" With a second version produced,

Pass Over was once again preserved, this time as a published script.

. . . Nwandu is presenting a third version of *Pass Over* for the Broadway run – one that provides medicinal hope in its ending. "It is an invitation to every Black person to experience the Promised Land," says Nwandu. "It's to give a taste of the new world. We need to provide the vision so we can fix the problems. It really is healing work."

. . . With *Pass Over*, what began as Nwandu's artistic snapshot responding to a specific time in history has expanded into a flipbook that captures new angles and lenses. It's up to us as a society to determine what's in the next frame.[2]

Overview

In rare instances, playwrights might opt for a democratic resolution and let the theatre company decide how their production will end.

The "Write What You Know" Conversation

Regardless of the theme or idea, it is important to recognize that the play you write will be an expression of you. What you think, question, observe, or are passionate about will ultimately be reflected in the play you write.

I'm often asked if you should "write what you know." This is an old adage which has been misinterpreted as a writing rule.[3] The literal interpretation of "write what you know" unnecessarily limits the stories we can tell both individually and as a community. Those limitations diminish the art form.

While you can write what you know, you do not have to do so. There are many reasons playwrights choose subjects for their work, including:

- They see a piece of art that excites them and makes them want to write about what it represents or says to them.
- They are politically and socially engaged and want to share their point of view on an issue or situation.
- They are curious about a topic and thoroughly research it to find something they want to write about.

In many plays, characters come into conflict because they have different backgrounds, and that has led to different ways of seeing the world. Their differences are the foundation for smart, compelling, dynamic plays. So, it would be impossible for a writer's identity to include all of these different experiences.

However, when you write characters whose experiences you are not directly connected to, you have a responsibility to take steps to educate yourself so that you tell those stories honestly and well. Steps you must take include, but are not limited to:

- Doing research;
- Engaging cultural consultants; and
- Inviting critiques about your representation of those characters from people who live and work in those communities.

This way, you will make sure that you are writing a deeper truth and don't slip into stereotype or appropriation*.

For example, the conflict in playwright Chisa Hutchinson's play *Somebody's Daughter* requires the characters to have different backgrounds in order to explore the themes Hutchinson is interested in exploring.

In *Daughter*, Alex is a brilliant but conflicted 15-year-old girl going to extremes to get her own mother to notice her. She's a parent's dream child – except her parents wish she was a boy. Luckily, she finds a sympathetic ear in Kate, her irreverent guidance counselor, who tries to help her cope with her difficult parents. The six characters in this play have different backgrounds and identity characteristics; they are different ages and races and have different experiences and professions. The differences in their identities and their experiences activate and elevate the drama because they are coming at questions of identity, race, and family relationships from different points of view. These differences help make it a compelling play.

Here are Hutchinson's thoughts on "writing what you know":

> People ask me all the time (because I'm a queer black female writer) if I think it's okay for people to write characters that belong to a demographic that isn't their own. And my response is basically, "I hope the hell so. Otherwise, what's the point of theater?" BUT! If you do it, you gotta be respectful about it. First of all, do you even know anyone who belongs

to the demo your outsider ass is trying to portray. If not, then please ask yourself why you feel compelled to do it. And find someone who belongs to that group to consult. Compensate them for their time. Read the work of insiders who have already repped their people because they've likely done it better than you will. Then brace for criticism. It's coming. But if your intentions are good, let that serve as a balm.[4]

While you don't want to limit yourself to "write what you know," it can be useful to draw from personal experience to write your own story or connect with what your character is experiencing.

For example, in my play *The Arsonists*, a father-daughter arson team sets fires for profit. One of the fires rages out of control, the father is killed, and the daughter drags his remains back to their cabin, burying him beneath the floorboards.

In her grief, she sings a song they shared, which summons his ghost. He rises from the floorboards, and they spend the play reckoning with their relationship, which was cut unexpectedly short. In the end, the daughter has processed her grief and moves forward with her life. Her father sinks back beneath the floorboards, peacefully laid to rest. Now. . .

- My father is alive.
- We do not set fires for a living.
- I cannot sing.
- We don't live in a cabin.
- I've never summoned someone from the dead.

Many of the elements of my play are entirely fictional. However, my father was seriously ill, and I was afraid of losing him. This generated many feelings and fears about his potential death. So, when writing the play, I tapped into those emotional responses to help me understand the character's emotional states.

However, for my play *Babel* about genetic testing and parents' rights, I had no emotional connection at first. I read an article about reproductive technology, which I found intellectually stimulating. So, I researched the technology, created characters who would be impacted by that technology, and slowly built a play world around them. Eventually, I did engage emotionally with my characters, but my initial connection with the play was intellectual.

While I did not literally "write what I know" to create either of those pieces, as my writing evolved, I became intimately familiar with the characters and their situations. They *became* what I knew because I did the purposeful work of research and reflection.

When you decide to "write what you know" directly, the play will still only be a theatrical representation of reality. While the details of the actual event are important, what's more important is that you use those details as a jumping-off point to craft your play.

When writing autobiographically, Playwright Matt Schatz[5] of *The Burdens* suggests:

> If you're writing an autobiographical play, make your protagonist unlikable. Writing teachers may tell us to 'write what we know,' and we all like to think

we know ourselves. And so we say, I'll write about this thing that happened to me. The problem is, in life is that things happen to you, but in a play, you (the protagonist) have to make something happen. The protagonist makes a decision, and most often, it's the wrong decision. It's sometimes hard for us to admit we've made the wrong choices in life, but the 'wrong choices' is a vital part of writing a play. So, whether you're writing about yourself, a character loosely based on yourself or someone you know, or someone entirely made up, make them mess up and do bad and even unlikable things. And if this is too difficult, think about not making your character the protagonist – maybe they're the antagonist. My play, *The Burdens*, is a brother-and-sister play loosely based on my sister and me. Mordy, the brother character, is an immature doofus who desperately wants to be an artist and is woefully inept with women; some things are far too embarrassing to make up."

Whether or not you "write what you know," the goal is to create a compelling piece of theatre.

Overview

You do not have to literally "write what you know," but you do have a responsibility to write what you write well and respect your characters, their communities, and situations. You can use your own feelings and experiences to inform how you write your play.

Resources
Student Favorites

The plays listed here were some of my students' favorites for illustrating the lessons in this chapter.

- *The Mountaintop* by Katori Hall (Methuen)
  - The night before his assassination, King retires to room 306 in the now-famous Lorraine Motel after giving an acclaimed speech to a massive church congregation. When a mysterious young maid visits him to deliver a cup of coffee, King is forced to confront his past and the future of his people.

- *The Thanksgiving Play* by Larissa FastHorse (Theatre Communications Group)
  - A group of well-intentioned white teaching artists scramble to create an ambitious "woke" Thanksgiving pageant. Despite their eager efforts to put on the most culturally sensitive

show possible, it quickly becomes clear that even those with good intentions can be undone by their own blind spots.

- *The Ugly One* by Marius von Meyenburg (On Stage Press/Soho Rep)
  - An absurd comedy in which Lette is a talented engineer, but his boss won't let him go to a conference to present his idea because of how he looks.

Additional Resource

- Playwrights on narrative: youtu.be/fGRyP3p-YPI?si=5ili9K08ELO4ONiO (National Theatre/London)

Discussed in Chapter

- *The Arsonists* by Jacqueline Goldfinger (Concord Theatricals)
- *Babel* by Jacqueline Goldfinger (Theatrical Rights Worldwide)
- *The Beauty Show* by Tyrfingur Tyrfingsson (Nordic Drama Corner)
- *The Burdens* by Matt Schatz (Theatrical Rights Worldwide)
- *Cinderella* (Disney film, 1950)
- *Pass Over* by Antoinette Nwandu (Concord Theatricals)
- *Somebody's Daughter* by Chisa Hutchinson (Dramatists Play Service)

Notes

1 Printed with permission of playwright, 2024.
2 "Why Antoinette Chinonye Nwandu Rewrote *Pass Over*'s Ending for Broadway," by Felicia Fitzpatrick, *Playbill.com*, 2021, https://playbill.com/article/why-antoinette-chinonye-nwandu-rewrote-pass-overs-ending-for-broadway.
3 "Write What You Know." This is a quote from *The Adventures of Tom Sawyer and Adventures of Huckleberry Finn* by Mark Twain. Twain did not say it was a rule for writing. It was written as dialogue for characters who do not know much about the world.
4 Printed with permission of playwright, 2024.
5 Printed with permission of playwright, 2024.

12
Point of View

Every play has a point of view that originates with the playwright. Sometimes, you know what the point of view of your play will be at the beginning of the writing process, and sometimes, you discover it along the way.

The Point of View of Your Play

Your point of view shapes your story. There is no objective point of view. Playwrights can write plays with very similar plots and stories yet still write unique work because every person's point of view is different.

Your point of view comes through particularly clearly in the story you chose to tell as well as the themes you chose to highlight. It exists on every page of your play. There are many ways your point of view affects your play, including, but not limited to:

- What story you choose to tell. (For example, if you're telling the story of a social conflict, are the protestors considered "rioters" or "justice seekers"? "Rioters" connotes criminal behavior. "Justice seekers" connotes a noble cause.)

- What themes, ideas, morals, and other conclusions your play draws. (For example, does love save the day? Does worshiping wealth cause the downfall of civilizations? Are Kings better than Presidents or Prime Ministers?)
- What characters you choose to tell the story with. (For example, who is the villain? Who is the hero? Who is the anti-hero? Are there even villains and heroes? Which characters are the "most" wrong and which are the "least" wrong at the end of the play?)

Since we are elevating an experience above other experiences by putting it onstage and focusing the audience's attention on it, your point of view on the story will be important.

Overview

Your Point of View is your superpower. It's what gives plays with similar situations, characters, or themes their own unique energy and life. Use your superpower wisely.

The Danger of a Single Story

Writer Chimamanda Adichie's TED Talk, *The Danger of a Single Story,*[1] is required viewing in all of my workshops. She talks about her life growing up in Nigeria and offers examples of how her limited knowledge of a person led to a reductive view of their lives. In one instance, she tells the story of Fide's Family:

So the year I turned eight we got a new house boy. His name was Fide. The only thing my mother told us about him was that his family was very poor. My mother sent yams and rice, and our old clothes, to his family. And when I didn't finish my dinner my mother would say, "Finish your food! Don't you know? People like Fide's family have nothing." So I felt enormous pity for Fide's family.

Then one Saturday we went to his village to visit, and his mother showed us a beautifully patterned basket made of dyed raffia that his brother had made. I was startled. It had not occurred to me that anybody in his family could actually make something. All I had heard about them was how poor they were, so that it had become impossible for me to see them as anything else but poor. Their poverty was my single story of them.

By working to create character specifics, explore their worlds, understand their conflicts, and do writing prompts and exercises, you help avoid the trap of writing a single story of a character or community.

Overview

As you write and revise, think: Am I being true to this character, is this story true to this character, or am I only thinking in "single story" terms? The more specific you are with a character, the truer that character becomes. The truer the character, the more powerful your play.

Visual Elements

Visual elements of theatre – like costume design, set design, and puppetry – can underscore your point of view.

Here's an example of using puppetry to express an artist's point of view. Playwright-Director-Creators like Jerrell Henderson of *AmericanMYTH: Crossroads* began their creation process thinking about the potential of puppetry to tell the story:

> When creating a puppet piece, my first question is, "Why Puppetry?" There are so many other forms of creative visual expression, it is important to understand what one values about the form of puppetry in general as well as the specific style of puppetry they wish to use or whether it will be a blend of styles. These questions encourage one to state clearly the driving idea of the piece (point of view).
>
> Beyond this, consider and then detail some form of basic visual imagery (storyboard) in order to detail how one believes the ideas they wish to communicate can be activated throughout the piece. There is no rule which states the piece must be a traditional narrative (beginning, middle, and end). However, it is essential that there be enough accessibility in the ideas being presented and the way in which the ideas are being presented, for the audience to latch on to draw understanding. It's a lot of trial and error and requires great focus, dedication, and patience.
>
> When creating my original shadow play, *AmericanMYTH: Crossroads*, performed at Free Street Theatre

in Chicago, IL, I knew that large scale, cinematic shadow puppetry was an essential ingredient to how the story must be told. My attraction to theatre in general lies within my curiosity with manipulating metaphor for the purposes of uncovering deeper truths behind everyday interactions. I view puppetry as pure metaphor. My exploration centered on getting the most visual metaphor out of images created and projected. More images, less language.

Also, large scale shadow theatre allows for more potential when it comes to creating a collage of images. I knew this was important to me, what I wanted to say about American folk/story traditions and how I wanted to say it.[2]

Overview

Visual elements also highlight the point of view of the play, so they are important to consider both in the writing process and as you move into production.

Check-In

If you are using this book to write a full play, before moving on to the next chapter, make sure that you have an initial story or overall idea of what might happen in your play. Spend more time fleshing out the Play World both narratively and with images. Make a list of possible themes/ideas of your play based on your characters and their opposition.

Resources

Student Favorites

The plays listed here were some of my students' favorites for illustrating the lessons in this chapter.

- *Life is a Dream* by Pedro Calderón de la Barca (Penguin)
  - This 17th-century allegory considers themes of free will and predestination, illusion and reality.

- *Chicken & Biscuits* by Douglas Lyons (Dramatists Play Service)
  - This comedy asks, "can rivaling sisters Baneatta and Beverly bury their father without killing each other? When a shocking family secret reveals itself, the two sisters are faced with a truth that could either heal or break them.

- *Queen Goneril* by Erin Shields (Playwrights Canada Press)
  - In this unique approach to adaptation, set seven years before *King Lear, Queen Goneril* centers the struggles of Lear's daughters as they negotiate patriarchal systems built to keep them relegated to the sidelines.

Additional Resource

- *Theatrical Mustang* podcast hosted by Woodzick features interviews by artists who often create more avant-garde or edgy theatre (available on major podcast outlets)

Discussed in Chapter

- *AmericanMYTH: Crossroads* by Jerrell Henderson
- *The Arsonists* by Jacqueline Goldfinger (Concord Theatricals)
- *Babel* by Jacqueline Goldfinger (Theatrical Rights Worldwide)
- *The Danger of a Single Story* by Chimamanda Adichie (TED Talk/youtu.be/D9Ihs241zeg?si=pHe D2cnfbVSxkR9_)

Notes

1 *TedTalks*, https://www.ted.com/talks/chimamanda_ngozi_ adichie_the_danger_of_a_single_story?subtitle=en, 2009.
2 Printed with permission of artist, 2024.

13

Scenes

Scenes are the building blocks of a play. A play can have multiple scenes or be one long scene. Regardless, the "scene" is how we organize stage time.

What Is a Scene?

A scene is a unit of stage time where something happens that the audience can perceive, and that adds meaning to the piece.

Let's break that definition down:

A Scene is a Unit of Stage Time

Scenes can be long or short; they can take two hours or two minutes. The length of scenes varies depending on the needs of the piece. There are some plays that are all one long scene and some plays that have a dozen scenes. We use the word "scene" to help denote the different parts of a play. But, their length, structure, and content differ from play to play.

Where Something Happens

An action(s) occurs, but what that action(s) is varies from play to play. I like to call it "something happens"

 DOI: 10.4324/9781003505310-15

because a scene involves action, conflict, and more. Here are just a few examples of how "something happens" in a scene: The "something happens" can be an intellectual argument that evolves over the course of the scene. The "something happens" can be a movement from stillness to gesture, which signifies a change in character. The "something happens" can be a character trying to achieve a goal and then either achieving it or failing to achieve it – both of which prompt the next "something happens." In participatory/interactive theatre, the "something happens" can be directly inclusive of the audience members themselves. In addition, multiple "something happens" can occur in a scene – but a scene needs at least one thing to happen.

That the Audience Can Perceive

Whatever your "something happens" is – it should be perçeivable by the audience – even if in a way they only feel gently and don't understand intellectually (yet). Theatre requires an audience to be theatre; we write to share something with the world. So, the audience must be able to perceive that something is happening by experiencing it through one or more of their five senses (sight, smell, hearing, taste, touch).

And that Adds Meaning to the Piece

In this case, we are using the word "meaning" very broadly. Adding meaning to a piece can literally mean expressing a moral or imparting a lesson. But "adds meaning" can also be deepening our understanding of a character or their situation, offering questions that resonate with one another, and/or sharing information that leads to a different understanding of what is happening in the piece (either in that moment or later in the play). Beyond these few examples, there are innumerable ways that the scene can "add meaning" to the piece.

Sometimes, in an early draft, you don't know what that meaning is or will be. But, when it's time to revise, and you look back at what you've written, you'll be able to see different "meanings" emerge. In revision, you select which meaning(s) to either develop or discard.

Overview

A scene is a unit of stage time where something happens that the audience can perceive, and that adds meaning to the piece.

Writing Exercise

When "something happens" to a character and/or audience, one or more of their five senses are engaged: taste, hearing, sight, smell, touch. This exercise gives you a chance to practice intentionally including sensory experience in your work.

Read the following scene from *The Post Office* by Rabindranath Tagore (circa 1912, edited for length and clarity).

In the scene, Amal is sick, and his Uncle Madhav will not let him leave the house to engage with the outside world. Amal's plea to his uncle often revolves around his senses, the sights and sounds of the outside world. By illustrating Amal's yearning for the outside world through sensory descriptions, we better understand Amal and the conflict of the scene.

Act One Excerpt

[*Amal enters*]

Amal. Uncle!

Madhav. Hullo! Is that you, Amal?

Amal. Mayn't I be out of the courtyard at all?

Madhav. No, my dear, no.

Amal. See, there where Auntie grinds lentils in the quern, the squirrel is sitting with his tail up and with his wee hands he's picking up the broken grains of lentils and crunching them. Can't I run up there?

Madhav. No, my darling, no.

Amal. Wish I were a squirrel! – it would be lovely. Uncle, why won't you let me go about?

Madhav. Doctor says it's bad for you to be out.

Amal. How can the doctor know?

Madhav. What a thing to say!

Amal. Does his book-learning tell him everything?

Madhav. Of course, don't you know!

Amal [*With a sigh*] Ah, I am so stupid! I don't read books.

Madhav. Now, think of it; very, very learned people are all like you; they are never out of doors.

Amal. Aren't they really?

Madhav. No, how can they? Early and late they toil and moil at their books, and they've eyes for nothing else.

Now, my little man, you are going to be learned when you grow up; and then you will stay at home and read such big books, and people will notice you and say, "he's a wonder." . . . It would have been my saving if I could have been learned.

Amal. No, I would rather go about and see everything that there is.

Madhav. Listen to that! See! What will you see, what is there so much to see?

Amal. See that far-away hill from our window – I often long to go beyond those hills and right away.

Madhav. Oh, you silly! As if there's nothing more to be done but just get up to the top of that hill and away! Eh! You don't talk sense, my boy. Now listen, since that hill stands there upright as a barrier, it means you can't get beyond it.

Amal. Uncle, do you think it is meant to prevent your crossing over? It seems to me because the earth can't speak it raises its hands into the sky and beckons. And those who live far and sit alone by their windows can see the signal. But I suppose the learned people –

Madhav. No, they don't have time for that sort of nonsense. They are not crazy like you.

Study and Write

- Go through *The Post Office* scene. Underline the "sense" words; for example, "crunching" is sound, and "picking up the broken grains of lentils" is feel. Also, underline the descriptive words that draw pictures for your imagination; for example, "Wish I were a squirrel!"

· Now, spend ten minutes writing a scene with two characters: one of whom wants to go outside, and the other will not let them go. What senses can you engage in the scene? Try to use all five of them in your one scene.

Side Note: Often, sensory elements (taste, hearing, sight, smell, touch) are paired with similes* and metaphors* to make them even more evocative. For example, "Now listen, since that hill stands there upright as a barrier, it means you can't get beyond it." The playwright pairs the sense of sight with a simile: "hill stands there upright as a barrier" to give you a stronger visual image.

When you have writer's block, ask yourself what sensory element you can add to enhance the moment. This tactic gives you something to focus on implementing in your scene and gets you writing again.

Overview

Throughout this book, I will encourage you to engage with the world you are creating in tangible ways because theatre is tangible; it leaps off the page onto the stage.

How Many "Something Happens" in a Scene?

In a scene, one thing could happen, or multiple things could happen.

For example, one very clear "something happens" would be a scene where a daughter returns home: she walks through the door, hugs her mother, but her mother does not hug back.

Or, many "something happens" could happen in a scene.

For example, a brother and sister could fight over the butter dish; this leads the mother to fight with the father over who bought the butter dish, and then the maid is fed up with their terrible behavior, so she breaks the butter dish.

In addition, there could be many "somethings happening" on different levels of reality or consciousness.

For example, in *Lydia* by Octavio Solis, the character Ceci has brain damage and can no longer speak, but she still has a tenuous understanding of what is happening around her.

Many "somethings happen" in the family's realistic scene while Ceci sits motionless in the room. Her siblings fight and reach a new level of conflict, and family truths are revealed, which change your understanding of the story.

However, Ceci is also processing this new information in her altered state. The realistic family scenes pause, and Ceci speaks gorgeous monologues to the audience. These monologues show us her point of view of what's happening in the realistic family scene, as well as back-story about the family's history. These non-realistic monologues shape the audience's understanding of the family drama.

The number of "something happens" in a scene depends on the type of story you are telling.

For example, changing the sequence of your scenes – what scene comes first, what scene comes next, and so on – can change the meaning of your piece. You can create additional meaning and layer added complexity into your play by playing with different scene sequences.

If you are ever having trouble writing a play, separate your scenes and move them around; does a different sequence work better? Are there some scenes you don't need or some ideas for scenes you should write to include in the play? Give yourself the freedom to play with your scenes and scene sequences.

Group Exercise

The goal of this exercise is to give the group a chance to have some fun and learn about the importance of scene sequences while making something together.

- Pick an image that includes pictures of people and share it with the group. The facilitator begins a scene with a one-sentence stage direction or piece of dialogue.
- Go around the room. Each person adds a sentence to the "scene" that extends the scene – the scene cannot reach an endpoint.

- After all the participants have spoken, then the facilitator concludes the scene.
- Discuss what scene might have come before the scene you created and what scene might have come after the scene you created.

The sequence of scenes can add new meaning to a piece.

Sometimes, a performer will ask you about their character's intention* in a scene. The character's intention is what a character wants in a scene and why they want it.

Overview

Today, in the myriad styles and forms of play-making we embrace, many things can happen in one scene or only one. The important thing is that something happens that the audience can perceive.

Check-In

Write a scene where your protagonist and antagonist meet. This scene may or may not end up in the play, but it will tell you a tremendous amount about their relationship.

Resources
Student Favorites

The plays listed here were some of my students' favorites for illustrating the lessons in this chapter.

- *Arcadia* by Tom Stoppard (Faber Drama)
  - In 1809, in a large country house sits Lady Thomasina Coverly, aged 13, and her tutor, Septimus Hodge. 180 years later, historian Hannah Jarvis and Bernard Nightingale stand in the same room to uncover the scandalous history of the home.

- *August: Osage County* by Tracey Letts (Theatre Communications Group)
  - A darkly comedic portrait of a dysfunctional Midwestern family at its finest – and absolute worst – centered around the disappearance of the family patriarch.

- *Love and Information* by Caryl Churchill (Theatre Communications Group)
  - A wide range of scenes connected by the themes of love and technology that can be arranged in different orders.

Additional Resource

- *Hey Playwright Podcast* by playwrights Tori Rice and Mabelle Reynoso is a conversational and very accessible podcast run by playwrights for playwrights. (heyplaywright.com)

Discussed in Chapter

- *Lydia* by Octavio Solis (Concord Theatricals)
- *The Post Office* by Rabindranath Tagore (translated by Devabrata Mukherjee/Project Gutenberg eBook 6523)

14

What's in a Scene

Scenes are the building blocks of a play, and the three main elements of a scene are goals, obstacles, and dramatic action.

Goals and Obstacles

In most scenes, each of your characters has at least one goal and one obstacle; there is something they want (goal), and something is keeping them from getting it (obstacle).

In *Little Red Riding Hood,* the Wolf's goal when chasing Grandma is to catch her and eat her. The obstacle is that Grandma does not want to be eaten, so she runs away and hides.

Goals and obstacles can be tangible (for example, winning the big game or marrying your soul mate) or intangible (for example, being comforted by a friend or having someone admit they are wrong.) Characters can have more than one goal and obstacle in a scene.

Dramatic tension – a state of uncertainty that often keeps the audience engaged in the performance – can be created by the push and pull of the goals and obstacles

DOI: 10.4324/9781003505310-16

in a scene. The audience wants to know – what is going to happen? Are they going to succeed or fail?

In early drafts, you might not know your character's goals and obstacles. That's okay. As you write and learn more about your characters, their inner workings will become clearer to you.

Here is an example of a direct goal and obstacle from the play *A Marvelous History of Mary of Nimmegen: Who for More Than Seven Year Lived and Had Ado With the Devil* written by an Anonymous playwright (circa 1515).

In this excerpt, Mary has gone to town to shop for her family. Night falls, and she is afraid of being robbed (or worse) walking home through dark woods that harbor wild animals, dangerous criminals, and the devil himself.

So, she seeks shelter with her aunt. But her aunt refuses to let her stay at her house because Aunt thinks Mary has been in town sinning all day. Aunt won't let a sinner into her house. This is an example of the main character having one very clear goal (get in the house for safety) and one very clear obstacle (Aunt will not let her in).

This combination of goal and obstacle creates dramatic tension: Will Mary get into the house and be safe overnight? Or will she have to stay outside and risk danger? The audience is intrigued to learn the outcome.

Here is the scene:

Mary approaches her aunt for shelter for the night.

MARY

Now have I all such as we wanted,
Bought and duly therefor paid.
But I have here so long delayed
That yonder is the night risen.
She stands outside her Aunt's house.
I see mine Aunt standing before her door.
In seemly wise I will her greet. –
She greets her Aunt.
Aunt, may Christ make all your sorrow sweet,
And all them you love keep both fair and well.

AUNT

Fy, welcome, devil, how do ye in hell?
Well, mistress, what would ye be hereabout?

MARY

For candles, mustard, vinegar and verjuice
And for such other as at home we have use;
It is grown so late; and little may it misease you
That as for tonight you make me a bed, if it please you.

The Aunt claims she has been sinning all day. Mary says that's not true.

AUNT

Chit! [*"chit" can mean perverted young woman*]
Not with your household matters since noonday!
You have not been busy, but sitting a-drinking
    [*drinking alcohol*]
In some snug corner with "fill the can, fill." [*having sex*]
And I have spoke with them too who would swear
They saw you and your own Uncle in such guise
All our kin you bring to scandal and shame.

Tush, vile progeny, you be too much to blame,
Out of my sight! You do mine eyes no good!

MARY

Lord God, what woe is mine in mood!
So vile reproach, such words of ignominy,
To hear and suffer, all unmerited!
Now, aunt, tell me if ye will make me a bed
For this one night?

AUNT

Be gone.

MARY

You do me wrong, Aunt.
Mary leaves her Aunt's house.

MARY

[*Now*] Under the trees I will make me a bed of leaves.
Walks into the woods, hides.
I reck not whom I meet, be it friend or kin,
Though the devil came in his own proper skin.
Under this hedge I will sit me down to rest,
Yielding myself, for ill or well,
To god or all the fiends of hell.

Mary's goal to find a safe place to stay for the night is thwarted by her aunt (the obstacle). In addition, the outcome pushes the story forward because Mary now has to find another way to remain safe throughout the night. What happens to her that night – because she couldn't sleep safely indoors – drives the story in a new direction.

A character's goals and obstacles can also be more subtle and lowkey.

For example, in *Birds of North America* by playwright Anna Ouyang Moench, scenes occur over a decade as a father and daughter struggle to reconnect. While the characters' stated goal is to bird watch, the real goal(s) are to wrestle with challenging aspects of their relationship and, hopefully, reconnect lovingly with one another.

In each scene, there is an external topic – approval of a wedding photographer, loss of a job – that they discuss, but we grow to understand that the topics of these conversations aren't as important as the real goal of slowly rebuilding their relationship. Their goals and obstacles are subtle and nuanced.

Or, the character's goal and obstacle might directly involve the audience.

For example, in the madcap comedy *all wear bowlers* by Rainpan43, two slapstick comedy actors accidentally "fall out" of an old black-and-white movie screen and are stuck onstage with you staring at them. They don't like you looking at them. So, they try to climb back into their movie screen but can't.

In the following scenes, they continue to try to avoid your gaze in different, incredibly funny ways. The main obstacle in most scenes is that they cannot figure out how to get back into their movie screen (where they will be able to avoid you).

The main goal and obstacle are the foundation of the show; it's why they can't leave the stage and end up performing for you. Once they figure out how to get back into the screen, the goal is achieved, the obstacle is over-come, and the show is over.

There are many ways to use goals and obstacles. Enjoy playing with what happens when you give your characters different goals or put new obstacles in their way. You'll learn a lot about them when you see how they handle different situations.

Overview

In early drafts, especially first drafts, goals and obstacles can sometimes feel forced because we don't know our characters well enough yet to truly name what they want and why they want it. However, keep writing. As you write, you learn more, and then you'll uncover what their real goals and obstacles need to be to fuel your play.

Dramatic Action

The dramatic action is the character going after their goal. Characters have multiple dramatic actions in a play.

You can use the term dramatic action to discuss a character going after their goal in a scene or through-out the play. For example, do they want to kiss someone? Kill someone? Trick someone? Do they want to win the big game or climb to the top of the mountain?

Sometimes, students get dramatic tension and dramatic action confused. So, here's a short review:

- Dramatic tension is a state of uncertainty that playwrights create in their work, often by setting up goals and obstacles. This tension helps keep the audience engaged. For example, will an athlete win the championship?

- Dramatic action is what a character does to achieve those goals; it's *how* they go after their goals. For example, the athlete buys extra sports equipment and spends extra time in practice to prepare for the championship.

Writing Exercise

Let's practice giving characters goals and obstacles.

Pick a character that you've created in other exercises. If you haven't created any characters yet, then pick a character you like from a play, TV show, or movie.

Take three minutes and brainstorm a list of goals that the character would like to achieve. These goals can be large (become President!) or small (brush their teeth without drooling on themselves).

Now, pick one of the goals. Who would be in opposition to those goals?

You now have two characters who are in opposition over a specific goal.

Take three minutes and brainstorm why one character wants to achieve the goal. Now, take three more minutes and dive deeper. What are some of the deeper, perhaps more emotional or deep-seeded reasons the character wants to achieve this goal?

Take three minutes and brainstorm why the other character wants to achieve the goal. Now, take three more minutes and dive deeper. What are some of the deeper, perhaps more emotional or deep-seeded reasons the character wants to achieve this goal?

Now, write a scene where the two characters meet in a private location. Each character is trying to achieve the goal, or part of the goal, and the other is an obstacle to that goal.

Read the scene. What did you learn about your characters? Are the goals you came up with in brainstorming what they really care about? Do they have other goals? Are they more passionate about other goals?

Sometimes, what you think a character's goals and obstacles will be – and what those goals and obstacles become as you write – can be different. So, don't be afraid to evolve your characters' goals and obstacles as you learn more about them and their world.

Overview

Dramatic action is the character going after what they want.

Stakes and Raising the Stakes

The stakes* of your play are what happens if a character fails or succeeds; this is the risk the characters take by making choices in the play.

The stakes fuel the audience's connection to the character because, generally, the audience cares whether or not the character fails or succeeds.

Throughout this series of obstacles and choices, we raise the stakes. "Raise the stakes*" means that we increase the risk of the actions that the character takes. Generally, when you raise the stakes, it is harder for your character to succeed.

By raising the stakes, we create more tension and conflict as we move forward in the character's journey.

A Raising the Stakes exercise from playwright Elyzabeth Wilder[1] of *Fresh Kills*:

When we talk about stakes, we are talking about what our character must lose and what they have to gain. The bigger the loss or the reward, the higher the stakes. If the stakes are high enough it will motivate our character to act, and we always want active characters. Something should be at stake in every scene and those stakes should be in some way connected to our character's ultimate goal. The easiest way to accomplish this is to create a ticking clock: what has to be accomplished before time runs out? What are the obstacles that must be overcome for this character to get what they want and how do those obstacles raise the stakes? In order to continuously raise the stakes, something has to change. Often the stakes grow and change as the characters grow and change. If the stakes are high and there are obstacles your character must overcome, then you audience will stay engaged.

Writing Exercise: Go through your play and at the top of each scene write the character's objective*. Then, highlight the obstacle that complicates their objective. Is it an obstacle they create, or is it an obstacle created by another character or an outside force? At the end of each scene write what has changed. Is that change a gain or a loss?

A few useful vocabulary words to know, if you don't already: objective, intention*, tactic*, and super-objective*.*

Overview

Stakes are what happens if your character fails or succeeds. Raising the stakes means that we increase the risk of the actions that the character takes.

Tone, Mood, and Atmosphere

Tone*, mood*, and atmosphere* are dependent upon the characters and their world. They are shaped by the dramatic action within your specific setting.

By atmosphere, we mean the overall feeling the play world itself projects. For example, in the madcap comedy *all wear bowlers,* the atmosphere is upbeat and bright, which supports the comedic journey of the characters. There are no bad things lurking in the corners of this piece; everything is bathed in a warm glow.

By tone, we mean the way the characters speak and move through the play world, which also contributes to the atmosphere. For example, in *all wear bowlers,* the characters are black and white film star clowns dressed like Charlie Chaplin. They create a humorous tone for the piece.

By mood, we mean how the piece makes you, the audience, feel. For example, *all wear bowlers* makes people feel happy. Mood may also refer to how we think the characters feel. So, if all that clowning makes us happy, it could be because we perceive the characters as happy.

The stakes are related to the atmosphere, tone, and mood of the piece because they, too, are defined by where you begin your process. For example, if you begin with the idea of writing a fast-paced comedy – like in *all wear bowlers* – then you know that the mood or feeling you want to evoke in your audience is laughter and joy.

Overview

The tone, mood, and atmosphere are dependent upon the choices the playwright makes about the characters and their world.

Timing, Pacing, and Rhythm

Timing* most frequently refers to the way characters interact. When a character is asked a question, do they reply quickly, pause to think, or share their head and then leave the stage? When a character sees someone doing something dangerous, do they jump in to help or say nothing while staring in disbelief?

Pacing* is the speed at which the play moves; it's how fast or slow information is revealed to the audience. For example, *all wear bowlers* is about slapstick and often quick comic timing, so it has a fast pace. But *Birds of North America* is a deep dive into the complex relationship between father and daughter; the characters are more hesitant to share, so it has a slower, more contemplative pace. The elements discussed previously – atmosphere, tone, and mood – all contribute to how the playwright will shape the pacing of the piece.

Rhythm* is slightly different from pacing but often connected to it. While pacing determines how fast or slow the narrative unfolds from moment to moment, rhythm is the overall flow of the narrative. The rhythm is determined by how the scenes, moments, music, and other elements are arranged to achieve an overall feeling of cohesion within the piece.

The rhythm of the piece often becomes clear later in the creation process – perhaps in draft three or five or even later in the life of the play. Since the rhythm is determined by the arrangement of elements of the play, then the right elements need to be present first before you can arrange them to create the overall flow, the overall rhythm, of the piece.

As you write, your dramatic action, stakes, atmosphere, tone, mood, rhythm, and pacing will become apparent – they are like puzzle pieces; once you understand how one fits into the puzzle of your play, then you can build around that understanding to fit the rest of the puzzle pieces together.

Overview

The tone, mood, and atmosphere, as well as the timing, pacing, and rhythm of a scene – and of a play – are dependent upon the choices the playwright makes about the characters and their world.

Resources
Student Favorites

The plays listed here were some of my students' favorites for illustrating the lessons in this chapter.

- *Everybody* by Branden Jacobs-Jenkins (Theatre Communications Group)
  - Inspired by the 15th-century morality play *Everyman*, the characters travel down a road toward life's greatest mystery and confront the inevitable.

- *Two Degrees* by Tira Palmquist (Theatrical Rights Worldwide)
  - Emma Phelps, a recent widow, is a paleoclimatologist focusing on ice in Greenland. When she's asked to testify at a Senate about climate change, the world begins to crack and shift underneath her feet.

Additional Resource

- Playwrights on scene writing: youtu.be/h03hyWV 8l7Q?si=1DT1alXXsn9LO742 (National Theatre/ London)

Discussed in Chapter

- *all wear bowlers* by Rainpan 43 aka Trey Lyford and Geoff Sobelle (filmed theatre piece/vimeo.com/ 34153466)
- *Birds of North America* by Anna Ouyang Moench (TRW Plays)
- *Fresh Killes* Elyzabeth Wilder (Methuen)
- *Little Red Riding Hood* based on a folktale by Valentina and Zinaida Semyonovna Brumberg (1937 short film/youtu.be/xb2vD2ovqE8?si=5rZi-WRreIB8ssQo)

Note

1   Printed with permission of playwright, 2024.

15

Scene Length and Scope

Scene length and scope depend entirely on how the scene is working within your play.

Scene Length

Scenes often vary in length to create a specific rhythm within the play itself. This rhythm strengthens the play overall because it supports, and often enhances, the themes and other elements of the play.

For example, perhaps you are writing a ghost story. The scenes might end right before the audience sees the ghost, so you build suspense and excitement until the ghost is finally revealed at the end of the play.

Another example, perhaps each scene is told from a different character's point of view. So, the scene length is dictated by how long it takes each character to give their perspective of the situation.

People often confuse length with form; as in, if it is a short scene, then it is a TV-style scene, and if it is a long scene, then it is a theatre-style scene. However, whether a scene is long or short in a play depends on many factors, including but not limited to action, conflict, scene location, rhythm, and pace, as well as the technical capabilities of the stage.

What is true is that film and television tend to be more plot-focused, meaning that they move from one scene to another scene as soon as new information is revealed. So, you tend to see more short scenes in film and television, but that's only because they are foregrounding moving the plot forward (often at a very quick pace).

Theatre tends to make more space for the emotional and psychological places where your character can go beyond what's required by the plot to move the story forward. The scenes are longer to make space for plot and story as well as dive into emotional and psychological depth. In addition, given the technology employed by film and television, storytellers can jump from one scene or moment to another very quickly and easily. Whereas, in theatre, we need time to transition on the stage in real time. So, the differing storytelling tools inform the piece.

Often, longer theatre scenes are messy in early drafts because they are so knotty and complex – but before you delete them, take time to work with them. These moments of complexity are often what set a good play apart from a great play.

In what follows, we'll explore several different scenes of varying lengths and how the length affects the play.

An example of effective long scenes is found in the farce *Noises Off* by playwright Micheal Frayn, in which people are running on and off stage for comedic effect. The long scenes allow the playwright to build the comedy to a fast and furious pitch without the interruption of a scene break. The stop-and-start nature of the scene break would ruin the rhythm of the comedy. The one long scene sustains the ongoing rhythm of the jokes, movements, and characters. It is one of the reasons the play is so funny.

One example of an effective short scene is the opening Prologue of *Romeo and Juliet* by William Shakespeare. It's less than a page, immediately thrusts us into a play world of conflict and strife, and the playwright teases us with beautiful language that hints at a decadent and powerful story. ("Ancient grudge"? "Star-crossed lovers"? "Death-marked love"? "Parents' rage"? – Yes, please! I need to know what's happening here.)

CHORUS

Two households, both alike in dignity
In fair Verona, where we lay our scene,
From ancient grudge break to new mutiny,
Where civil blood makes civil hands unclean.
From forth the fatal loins of these two foes
A pair of star-crossed lovers take their life;
Whose misadventured piteous overthrows
Doth with their death bury their parents' strife.
The fearful passage of their death-marked love
And the continuance of their parents' rage,
Which, but their children's end, naught could remove,
Is now the two hours' traffic of our stage;
The which, if you with patient ears attend,
What here shall miss, our toil shall strive to mend.

Notice that this excerpt is relatively plot and exposition-heavy. This is common in short theatrical scenes; they provide vital plot, story, and exposition that allow us to move on quickly to juicier scenes with more depth. However, they still include core elements like nods to conflict ("ancient grudge"), high stakes ("death-marked love"), and compelling stylized dialogue ("a pair of star-crossed lovers take their life").

If you are using a scene as an exposition dump – meaning, the only reason for the scene is to share backstory or other background information – then that scene might not need to exist. You can probably find ways to share that information in another scene or make the current scene more dynamic. We often include more exposition than required in early drafts as we are beginning to understand the piece. However, we sculpt and reduce that exposition as we write and revise. (If you are having difficulty with exposition then return to Chapter 8. Use those writing exercises to support your process.)

In addition to scenes varying in length, playwrights can leave the order in which the scenes are performed up to the artists staging the show. This is typically found more in experimental work.

For example, in *Love and Information* by Caryl Churchill, the play is a series of scenes which investigate our relationship to the overwhelming amount of information we can easily access thanks to technology (like social media). It asks where love and emotion – our full humanness – fits into our information-drenched daily lives. The play has seven sections. Each section is comprised of scenes. The seven sections must be performed in order; however, the scenes within each section can be performed in whatever order the artists wish. There is also a "random" section of scenes included at the end of the play that can be used anywhere within the play.

Much like Nwandu's "democratic resolution" choice in *Pass Over* (see Chapter 11), Churchill's choice in *Love and Information* acknowledges the relationship between artist and audience in a unique way; by giving the artists primary control over how to present the play depending upon how they want to connect with the audience.

Writing Exercise and Optional Group Exercise

This exercise gives you an opportunity to play with how scene length changes or focuses a scene.

- Pick your two favorite animals.
- Write a short one-page scene where they meet.
- Write a longer two-page scene where they meet (in the same way or a different way).
- Write an even longer four-page scene where they meet (in the same way or a different way).

Think about: How did the length of the scene change the content? How did it change the pacing of the scene? Did it change the pacing? Did it change the content?

If you are in a group, select one scene to revise. Read the scene aloud. Discuss the original draft and how the scene has evolved.

Overview

There is no right or wrong scene length. The length of the scene depends on what you're trying to do with it.

Writer's Block Prompt

Often, when we get stuck during our writing, it is useful to brainstorm a list of what could happen in the next scene. Next, cross off your brainstorming list of options that do not interest you. Now, pick one of the remaining ideas to write. You may or may not use this new moment in the final draft, but it will get you writing again.

The Scope of the Scene

There will be a point at which the audience begins engaging with the scene. A point at which they reach the middle of the scene. And a point at which the scene ends.

For every scene you share, the audience is going to make assumptions based on what you share with them: where you begin your scene, where it goes, and how it ends.

In *The Empty Space,* director Peter Brook says theatre "is like a magnifying glass and also like a reducing lens." When you put a scene onstage, you magnify a moment (or series of moments); you give them added importance by putting them onstage. However, you are *only* showing those moments, so you are drawing boundaries around a piece; those boundaries affect what you show the audience. What you show the audience affects how they perceive the piece. You are both magnifying and reducing at the same time. It's important to track and understand this because what you choose to leave in or out of your scenes impacts both the play and how the play is perceived in the larger world.

For example, in the fairytale *Cinderella*, you see the version of the story that centers on Cinderella and her plight, so you only see the stepmother's bad behavior. What if you also saw Cinderella slapping her before being banned from the ball? What if you saw the stepmother being told by an uncle that he would beat Cinderella if she left the house? How would that change how you feel about the stepmother barring Cinderella from going to the ball?

The choice you make about where you begin and end scenes teaches the audience what's important and how to draw meaning from it. Since a scene is just one part of the whole play, how the meaning of each scene builds on one another will influence how audiences understand the play.

For example, in *Dutchman*, playwright LeRoi Jones aka Amiri Baraka sets the play in a subway car for one subway ride. Into this setting, he brings Lula (a mature white woman) and Clay (a young black man).

By setting the play during one short subway ride, we only get to know Lula and Clay through their actions on that ride. This choice gives Jones the time and space to dive deeply into the racial conflicts both between and within the characters. This magnifies those conflicts, allowing us to explore their nuances so that we leave the theatre having experienced the explosive journey of Lula and Clay as well as engaging in a rigorous intellectual conversation.

However, like all choices, it has repercussions. This choice means that we're not going to see the lives and actions of the characters beyond the subway car. By not seeing their lives outside the subway car, we only draw meaning from the interactions we see inside the subway car. So, this choice "reduces" what we see of their lives even as it gives Jones space to "magnify" the complex conversation surrounding race in the U.S.

Group Exercise

This exercise gives participants an opportunity to practice magnifying/reducing themselves and see how others magnify/reduce the same piece of text as well. This will show the wide variety of ways that even a single piece of text can shape audience perceptions based on beginning and endpoints.

- Give participants a scene from a play – any scene will do, although, for emerging writers, it's often easier to begin with a scene that has at least one

clear conflict and distinct characters. All participants receive the exact same scene.

- Now, have the group read the scene aloud.
- Next, have the participants write quietly for 15
  minutes. During this writing time, they should
  reflect on the scene. Then, they should write either
  a new beginning or a new ending. So, they should
  expand the scene at the beginning or the end (not
  in the middle). If they have time, they should also
  write down why they chose to expand in the way
  they did and what impact they are hoping that
  expansion has on the audience.
- Now, read the scenes aloud. Discuss how changing the beginning and end points changes the
  understanding of the characters, situation, and
  themes of the piece. See if the expansions did/did
  not change the audience's perception of the scene
  in the way the playwright hoped it would.

Overview

*Be cognizant that when and where you begin
and end scenes, what you share in the scene
and exclude from it shapes the audiences' perception of the piece and the conversation surrounding it.*

Resources

Student Favorites

The plays listed here were some of my students' favorites for illustrating the lessons in this chapter.

- *The Piano Teacher* by Julia Cho (The Language Archive and Other Plays/Theatre Communications Group)

  - Mrs. K is an elderly widow who lives by herself in a small suburban town. One day, she finds herself compelled to call her old students, but is it out of loneliness or some other, darker need to know an untold truth?

- *Fuente Ovejuna* by Lope de Vega *(Three Major Plays*/Oxford University Press)

  - A 17th-century play based on the 1476 historical incident in Castile where villagers kill the military commander who mistreated them.

Additional Resource

- *Six Perfections* blog by playwright-screenwriter Aurin Squire is an enjoyable mix of conversations about art, submission opportunities, and reflections on the world. (sixperfections.blogspot.com)

Discussed in Chapter

- *Dutchman* by LeRoi Jones aka Amiri Baraka (Harper)
- *Noises Off* by Michael Frayn (Concord Theatricals)
- *Romeo and Juliet* by William Shakespeare (Folger Library/online)

16

Structure and the Dramatic Question

Structure is the organizing principle of your play. There are many types of structures and many ways of organizing your play. The Dramatic Question is an element that helps define your play's structure.

Before We Begin: Dramaturgy

The word "dramaturgy*" will be mentioned multiple times in this chapter. Overall, dramaturgy is the study of how a play works, why it works, and how the play works for the audience. In this chapter, when playwrights talk about the "dramaturgy" of their play, they are specifically talking about the structure of their play and how that informs both their process as well as how the audience perceives the play.

What Is Structure?

Structure is the organizing principle of your play. It helps you organize scenes and moments in your play. This organization helps you refine your characters, plot, story, and other elements so you can share them with the audience. Your structure helps create a shared understanding between the artist and audience of the

216   DOI: 10.4324/9781003505310-18

context of the play and how to understand it. Structure also creates meaning within your play by shaping content, form, and style.

Let's break that down:

Structure is the organizing principle of your play. It helps you organize scenes and moments in your play.

What does that actually mean? Let's use a cooking metaphor:

When you make a meal, you organize your kitchen. You pull out the pots, pans, and ingredients you'll need. Eventually, you'll organize these items – perhaps cooking ingredients in a pan at a specific temperature for a specific amount of time – so that the result is the meal you intended to make and share with your family. The organization and process of meal-making are tied directly to how the meal turns out and is consumed.

Just like you organize your kitchen to make a meal for your family, you organize your play to create a piece of art and shape how it is understood by audiences.

Sometimes, you know the structure beginning with the first draft; other times, you need to write a draft (or two or three) before you know how your play needs to be organized.

This organization helps you refine your characters, plot, story, and other elements to share them with the audience.

To continue with the cooking metaphor: You might have many different types of pots and pans to cook with and many ingredients to choose from, but to cook the specific meal you intend, you must select the right elements for that moment.

In playwriting, this means you generate a lot of material when working on a play: characters, locations, dreams, moments of realization, and more. Much of what you generate in your process, especially early on, will never make it to the stage. So, of everything you generate, what will the audience see onstage? What will they not see onstage? How will you organize the vast amount of material you generate?

Your structure helps create a shared understanding between the artist and audience of the context of the play and how to understand it.

To continue with the cooking metaphor: What type of meal are you making? Is it Indian food or Mexican food? Is it spicy or mild? By defining the type of food you are cooking, your family knows how to appreciate it. They know that if you're making roti, then they should eat it one way – they should not expect to eat it like an apple or a hamburger or for it to taste like an apple or hamburger. Giving your family a general idea of what you're making creates an understanding of why and how they should consume it. All of the members of your family do not have to agree on how it tastes – but they at least understand the context of how it should be consumed.

In playwriting, this means structure is a tool that helps create a shared general understanding of the work so we can all be in conversation with each other about it. Now, art is subjective. As such, artists and audiences often have different points of view on the same piece of art. And that's great! It's one reason art is interesting. All the members of an audience will not all have the same opinion about a piece of work – but at least understand the general context of the piece, so they have a starting place for conversation about it. The structure can help the playwright's stories and ideas reach as many audience members as possible.

> *Structure helps create meaning within your play by shaping content, form, and style.*

To continue with the cooking metaphor: When you cook, you organize food in different ways to create different flavor combinations. You might chop red peppers into small pieces for a salsa, but slice them in thick wedges for a salad. Both ways of preparing the peppers are right for what you want to do with the pepper.

Structure is the same way. You can bend, reshape, slice, and dice your structure to create new meanings or highlight inherent meanings within your play.

When we put it together, we get the definition: *Structure is the organizing principle of your play. It helps you organize scenes and moments in your play. This organization helps you refine your characters, plot, story, and other elements so you can share them with the audience.*

Your structure helps create a shared understanding between the artist and audience of the context of the play and how to understand it. Structure also creates meaning within your play by shaping content, form, and style.

Before we dive into specific structures in the next chapter, here are two examples that give you an overall sense of how play structure affects a work of art:

- Organizing your play as a straightforward narrative where the characters move from beginning to end in a lifelike fashion.

  - In playwright Lillian Hellman's *The Little Foxes,* the main character, Regina, is a woman who wants to become wealthy and powerful in her community but cannot do so on her own because social conventions leave women powerless. So, she decides to fight her brothers and manipulate her husband to get ahead.

  - The scenes of the play occur chronologically back-to-back or in the same order as everyday life, where characters make choices and move forward. By the end of the play, Regina has gained wealth and a high social standing in her community. Hellman uses a straightforward chronicle of Regina's experience to show the realistic social constraints she struggles against.

- Organizing your play around a theatrical element – like a monologue.

  - In playwright Harmon dot aut's play *Tornado Tastes Like Aluminum Sting*, they choose to

organize their play around a series of mono-
logues spoken directly to the audience. In
Tornado, the main character, Chantal, is on the
Autism Spectrum.

- A tornado hits Chantal and their parents' home.
  Chantal is trapped under the debris, and while
  they wait to be rescued, they cope by reliving
  their family story.

- To make the journey of this neurodivergent
  main character more accessible to neurotypical
  audience members, it alternates between scenes
  between characters (who only speak to one
  another, as if there is a Fourth Wall* between us
  and them) and monologues by Chantal, the
  main character, speaking directly to the audience. In these monologues, Chantal explains
  how their neurodivergence shapes their perspective of the world at that moment. This way,
  neurotypical audience members have a deeper
  understanding of what Chantal is going through
  in the more traditional scenes.

- This structure allows the playwright to create a
  piece that is true to their character while helping
  audience members engage with the play since
  the point of view of the character telling the
  story might be different than anything the audience ever encountered.

In these examples, the structure helps organize scenes
and moments so that the intent of the story, as written
by the playwright, is made clear.

Structure as Guiding Principle from playwright Kareem Fahmy of A Distinct Society:

Let's say you're early in the first draft of a new play. Maybe you have a strong (or not so strong) idea of where the play is going. You've got characters, a plot, thematic principles to help move you forward, but then you get lost in that messy middle. Things aren't working and you feel stuck. This is where I urge you to look at structure.

Conceptualizing a play from a structural point-of-view can be of tremendous benefit to your process. It can keep you on track in those "I just don't know what I'm doing" moments. It can help unlock style and theatrical form. And theatre history is full of dramaturgical structures you can refer to, reinvent, or remix based on the needs of your play.

My play *A Distinct Society* borrowed the four-act, real-time structure of Chekhov but compressed into 95 minutes. The limitation of knowing that each scene was continuous action with a time lapse in between helped reveal to me what the play was doing.

I struggled several aimless drafts of my play about NCAA women's basketball, *American Fast*, before realizing that I could structure the play into six "rounds" corresponding to March Madness. I then incorporated a direct-address prologue that helped launch the play as a sporting event. Applying this structural conceit helped give the play the momentum it needed.

> It's easy to think of dramaturgy as something that you study or analyze, but as a playwright you are building a house that you hope will stand forever. Your structure is the foundation of that house.[1]

Overview

Structure is the organizing principle of your play. It helps you organize scenes and moments in your play. This organization helps you refine your characters, plot, story, and other elements so you can share them with the audience. Your structure helps create a shared understanding between the artist and audience of the context of the play and how to understand it. Structure also creates meaning within your play by shaping content, form, and style.

The Perfect Structure?

There is no such thing as a "perfect" structure. There is only finding a structure that works for your play. Sometimes, you will know that structure from the start of the writing process. Other times, the structure might evolve throughout writing and revision.

Overview

There is no such thing as a perfect structure for all plays; the structure of your play depends on its creative needs. But, by studying the

---

> *structure of other plays and practicing different structures, you will have a better understanding of the structure that is right for your plays in the future.*

Dramatic Question

The Dramatic Question(s) is the overarching tension of the play and is tied to the main characters' conflicts.

The dramatic question can also influence structure. Since structure helps your audience understand the play, and the Dramatic Question gives your play its powerful dramatic engine, then they both influence one another.

Usually, the dramatic question is made clear at the beginning of the play regardless of the play's structure. These questions might morph and shift during the play or not. These questions might or might not be answered by the end of the play.

Some people think that only dramas – serious plays – have dramatic questions. But actually almost every play has a dramatic question regardless of style, tone, or genre. Sometimes dramatic questions are clearly stated, sometimes they are only implicitly referenced, but since we are watching a character do something there will always be a question of whether or not they succeed in doing that thing. Plays have one or more dramatic questions. Here are a few examples of dramatic questions:

- In *Romeo and Juliet,* a main dramatic question is, "Will Romeo and Juliet live happily ever after?"
- In *The Little Foxes,* a main dramatic question is, "Will Regina be able to find the wealth and happiness she desires?"
- In *Tornado Tastes Like Aluminum Sting*, two main dramatic questions are, "Will Chantal survive this disaster and will they reconnect (physically, emotionally, and spiritually) with their parents?"

The Dramatic Question(s) don't need to be fully answered by the end of the play, but it's important to know:

(1) Are you answering that question(s) by the end of the play?
(2) If you are not answering that question, why?
(3) How does the dramatic question influence the way your audience receives the play?

Sometimes, a playwright knows the Dramatic Question at the beginning of the writing process, but often, they do not, or the Dramatic Question shifts as they write.

Personally, I like to go into my first draft with an idea of what the Dramatic Question could be for the play. This gives me a general "answer" to the Dramatic Question to aim for in my writing. However, as I write drafts and get to know my characters better, I might discover other Dramatic Question(s) that are more important to them. So, I might discard my original Dramatic Question and use one that has emerged.

Overview

The Dramatic Question is the overarching tension(s) of the play. Dramatic Questions are an integral part of most plays regardless of the structure you use.

Writer's Block prompt from playwright Migdalia Cruz of El Grito Del Bronx *on using your imagination and all your senses to conjure your characters.*

Since I began my studies with María Irene Fornés and her "Method writing," I have found that writer's block is rare indeed. I have learned that there are more ways to write than with a pen and paper. Writing is thinking, breathing, listening to your characters' music, thoughts and taste.

Becoming aware of the light in the rooms that they inhabit. Take the time to imagine what they see when they look out their window – or what they cannot see. When you begin to feel stuck with a character, take your character on a date – to the movies, a museum, a concert. What is your character's favorite artist and why? Perhaps the character knows nothing about Art but knows what they are attracted to and why. This is valuable information for the back story of your character. You could also just stay at home and play music that you imagine they would like as you cook or clean or read through their lines. Avoid pressuring yourself and the character to fit a scene or say things you want them to say. Just be with them. Breathe with them.

See and hear the world as they do. That's an essential part of a writer's job, and you will banish the block. Stop trying to be a writer, and just allow the words to emerge from the character – and write that down. That's learning how to tell your truth.[2]

Check-In

If writing a play as you move through this book, brainstorm possible dramatic questions for the play.

Resources
Student Favorites

The plays listed here were some of my students' favorites for illustrating the lessons in this chapter.

- *The Fever* by Wallace Shawn, a one-character play (*Wallace Shawn Plays 1*/Faber)
    - The nameless narrator lies ill and alone in a dreary hotel room in a poverty-stricken country. He struggles with memories and his own conscience, which are challenged by the misery and poverty he sees.

- *The Arsonists* by Jacqueline Goldfinger, a two-character play (Concord Theatricals)
    - A lyrical and darkly funny play with music about the eternal bond between parent and child, centered around a father-daughter arson team.

- *Death and the Maiden* by Ariel Dorfman, a three-character play (Penguin)
  - Is Gerardo and Paulina's new friend the same man who raped and tortured her as she lay blindfolded in a military detention center years before? Who is he really, and what does that mean for her life?

Additional Resource

- The *Arts Calling* podcast hosted by Jaime Alejandro Cruz features casual conversations with theatre-makers about their life stories. (artscalling.com)

Discussed in Chapter

- *A Distinct Society* by Kareem Fahmy (Dramatists Play Service)
- *El Grito Del Bronx* by Migdalia Cruz (No Passport Press)
- *The Little Foxes* by Lillian Hellman (Dramatists Play Service)
- *Romeo and Juliet* by William Shakespeare (Folger Library/Online)
- *Tornado Tastes Like Aluminum Sting* by Harmon dot aut (New Play Exchange)

Notes

1 Printed with permission of playwright, 2024.
2 Printed with permission of playwright, 2024.

17

Five Popular Structures

Structure is the organizing principle of your play. There are many types of structures, and we will explore five of them in this chapter.

Popular Structures: Well-made, Episodic, Circular, Pattern, Ritual

While structures can look many ways, there are a few popular structures that you are likely to encounter. These structures evolved over time based on a wide range of factors, including cultural practices, what artists thought audiences wanted to see, and the physical location of where plays were being produced.

We will look at these five popular structures:

- Well-made
- Episodic
- Circular
- Pattern
- Ritual

Plays can use these structures, use elements of these structures, or have other structures entirely.

I recommend writers spend time practicing different structures in their purest form; for example, can you write a piece that only uses elements of the well-made structure? Or does it only use elements of the pattern structure? Like any skill, once you get the basics down, you are better equipped to use that skill again or use that skill as a jumping-off point for something new.

(1) Well-made Play Structure

A well-made play is the most popular structure in American theatre. These plays are about what happens next in a character's life; one event follows another that follows another until the end of the play.

In a well-made play, there is a very clear beginning, middle, and end to a character's journey. At the beginning of the journey, a character behaves one way. In the middle of the journey, a character learns more about themselves and the world. At the end of the journey, the character changes (often becoming better or smarter in some way).

Let's break that journey down into smaller steps:

The Beginning (usually 10–15% of the play)

Status Quo

At the beginning of the play, we see the character in their status quo* – meaning we see them in their everyday life as it existed before the play began. Their journey is about to begin.

For example, in the beginning of "Cinderella," we see her cleaning her family home and being treated poorly. We understand that this is her everyday life.

Inciting Incident*

Then, their status quo is broken by an inciting incident. The inciting incident is something that happens to a character that is so challenging that they cannot just go back to their everyday status quo life. The introduction of the inciting incident requires them to make a new choice and sets them off on their journey.

In *Cinderella*, Cinderella learns that there is going to be a one-time-only ball, a type that she has dreamed of attending. She has one shot at attending – will she go? Yes! She decides to go. She is off on her journey to attend the ball.

The Middle (usually 75–85% of the play)

Rising Action*/Mounting Complications*

Now, we move into the middle of a character's journey. Throughout the middle of the play, the character faces obstacles to their goals.

When the character confronts an obstacle, they make a choice and try to overcome the obstacle. If they fail to overcome the obstacle, they must make a different choice that leads to another action (to get over or around the obstacle). If they succeed in overcoming the obstacle, then their success leads to an even larger obstacle.

Here is how the middle of *Cinderella* works:

- Cinderella tries many ways to get a beautiful dress for the ball but keeps getting thwarted.
- First, she tries to use her mother's old dress, but she doesn't have enough nice material.
- Second, she decides to take old jewelry and cast off the fabric that her stepsisters have discarded and use those to sew a nicer dress.
- Third, when she almost has a nice dress, her stepsisters give her more duties, so she doesn't have time to finish the dress.
- Now she must have help from her friends to finish the dress.
- In the end, the stepsisters discover she has used their cast-offs and rip her dress to shreds. Now, after facing all of those increasing obstacles, she is back at the beginning; she has no dress, but the ball is even closer.
- Will she find a solution in time to make it to the ball? (Eventually, she does reach the ball.)
- The middle continues as she faces more obstacles, creates more goals, and the stakes get higher and higher, threatening to overwhelm her so that she can't go to the ball.

Stakes and Raising the Stakes*

Throughout this series of obstacles and choices, we raise the stakes. Raising the stakes means that we increase the risk of the actions that the character takes. By raising the stakes, we create more tension and conflict as we move forward in the character's journey.

In *Cinderella*, when she borrows jewelry from her step-sisters without their permission, we are raising the stakes. She's made a choice that has a higher risk – getting caught and getting in trouble for stealing – but that risk also comes with a higher reward – having a much nicer dress.

Climax*

The climax is the point of highest tension in the story. It is the crescendo of the play where the protagonist makes a big decision based on what has happened and what they have learned, and then we see the immediate aftermath of that choice.

All the goals, obstacles, complications, and choices have led to the climax either directly or indirectly.

Often, the climax is tied to the theme of the play; whatever the character chooses to do – or actively not do – in the climax illustrates the theme of the play.

In *Cinderella*, she thinks that she wants to go to the ball, but really, once she gets there, not only does she enjoy the party but she also falls in love with the Prince. However, she is afraid of the consequences she will suffer if her family realizes that she disobeyed them and went to the party, so she flees the ball.

The Prince comes to the village to find her. However, in order for her to achieve her new goal of being with him, Cinderella has to reveal her deception to everyone – including her abusive family – in hopes that by identifying herself, then the Prince will then whisk her away from her family and they will live happily ever after. She risks the danger of revealing her true identity and the possibility that the Prince will not protect her from her family. (He does protect her and they live happily ever after.)

The choice the character makes at the climax connects with the theme of the play, showing us what a character has learned or not learned on their journey.

One theme in *Cinderella* is that it's worth taking a big risk to find true love. Cinderella's choice to reveal her true identity to her family and the Prince – therefore, risking her safety to find true love – exemplifies this theme. It is this theme in action.

If the character has changed thanks to what they've learned on their journey, that is called a "reversal" and is usually part of the climax. She has reversed the direction of her life.

In *Cinderella*, we see that Cinderella has been changed by her journey because she stands up for herself at the end of the play, something she was not able to do at the beginning of the play.

If the lessons that the character learns throughout their journey lead them to gain a new, deeper understanding, then that's called a "realization" and is usually part of the climax as well.

In *Cinderella*, she realizes that she is worthy of being seen and loved.

Usually, the climax and realization speak to the themes of the play, what the artist wants to discuss, exemplify, or share with the audience.

The End (usually 5–10% of the play)

Denouement*

In the denouement, we see how the story turns out. The term denouement is derived from a French word meaning "to unknot." We "untangle" the strands of the plot by resolving any lingering questions or conflicts. We usually see the character settle into a new status quo or, at least, understand the new direction their life is heading after this long journey.

For example, in *Cinderella*, Cinderella and the Prince marry and leave for their honeymoon.

Writing Exercise with Optional Group Component

Watch the short film *Little Red Riding Hood* based on a folktale by the Brumberg Sisters – or – use your own version. Identify the beginning, the middle, and the end of this narrative film.

Consider and/or discuss these questions:

- How would this story be different if told backward (end, middle, beginning)? How would that change/ not change our experience of the story?

- What would be our first impression of the characters if we began with the final scene? How would that impression shape/not shape our idea of who those characters are?
- How would this story be different if told only through the beginning and end, with nothing in the middle?
- How would that impact our understanding of the character's journeys?
- What would happen if we only saw the middle of the story, with no beginning or ending scenes?

The goal of playing with structure is not to come to a "right" answer but to understand how changing the well-made play structure impacts our understanding of the story.

Sometimes, the well-made structure is broken into acts to make it easier to understand and use the structure. Some teachers break the well-made play down into three, four, or five Acts – depending on their preference and how they teach. Just know that – no matter how many acts they say your well-made play should have, the structure is the same. They are simply different ways to break down the same elements of the structure to make the structure easier to use.

My favorite illustration of the well-made play structure is the children's book, *The Monster at the end of this Book,* by John Stone, illustrated by Mike Smollin. It's a fun way to show the structure in a quick 60-second read.

Overview

The well-made structure is a straightforward storytelling narrative popular in American theatre. A character goes on a journey to reach a goal. They encounter obstacles that require them to make choices, and those obstacles and choices lead to conflicts. This raises the stakes of the play. They face harder and harder decisions until they reach the climax of their story when they must make the hardest decision of all. This major decision determines whether the character succeeds or fails and how the story turns out. The themes of the play are usually clarified through this decision.

(2) Episodic

Episodic plays, as the name suggests, use a series of episodes to present the plot. In this context, an episode is an important moment in the story. Episodes are often shorter than scenes in a well-made play, although, like scenes, they can be any length. Episodes may contain less detail and may not directly connect with each other. Instead, they are tied together by character, action, or theme.

Here are the characteristics of an episodic structure:

- These episodes can feel disjointed in terms of the story they are telling – even if they are connected by theme, tone, place, or other unifying element.

- Usually, the episodes do not clearly tell the audience what happened between each scene to motivate the next scene.
- Instead, the audience must make deductions – and often large leaps in logic – to figure out what has happened between one scene and the next.
- Each scene is equally important.
- Sometimes, these scenes occur out of chronological sequence.
- Episodic plays usually show events that occur over a long period of time.
- An episodic play can feel like watching a highlight reel rather than an entire sporting event or discerning the way a collection of tiles creates an image in a mosaic.

For example, in playwright Sophie Treadwell's *Machinal*, we see the story of a young woman in 1920s U.S.A. who does everything society asks of her, but she's still unhappy. She has an affair with a younger man, which fuels her desire to live her own life. Eventually, she murders her husband to free herself, is convicted of the crime, and is executed in the electric chair.

Treadwell structures the play in episodic scenes:

- Scene 1: The woman is at work, hating the job and her life, but has no way out.
- Scene 2: At home with her mother, she is unhappy, so she decides to marry her boss in case that might make her happy.

- Scene 3: On her honeymoon where – even though she is now married – she is still not happy.
- Scene 4: Having given birth to their child, which she's told should make her happy, but she is still not happy.

These scenes continue until she is executed.

By using this structure, Treadwell gives us a cascading feeling of the young woman's epic plunge into despair, violence, and death. It also echoes the chaotic, out of control feeling the young woman experiences inside – this is a part of externalizing the character's interior life. (See Chapter 3 for externalization exercises.)

As we discussed earlier in the book, plays give the audience an experience of the moment or moments in a story. The structure you chose can help amplify that experience.

Writing Exercise

Take the *Little Red Riding Hood* folktale.

Make a list of the moments in Little Red's story.

Make a list of the possible themes of her story.

Select a theme.

Take your theme and select the moments that would help underscore the theme. Add any description of additional moments that you think would help underscore your theme.

> Organize the moments into an episodic structure and reflect on how they shift the story.
>
> *Episodic structure changes how you can play with elements like theme, character, space, and time.*

Overview

The episodic structure emphasizes individual moments that add up to the full picture of a story and, often, organizes the scenes around the theme.

---

(3) Circular

The circular structure is like the episodic one. However, the episodic usually leads to a conclusion of an event or journey (and often a concluding moral), while the circular structure begins and ends at a similar place so the play could immediately repeat itself.

Episodic plays give the audience a sense of finality, while circular plays give the audience a sense of inevitable return to (an often dreary) status quo that the characters cannot escape. So, the structure of the play (beginning and ending in the same place) often mirrors the dramatic action of the characters who start in one place and go on a journey, only to return to the same place.

For example, in Samuel Beckett's *Waiting for Godot*, Vladimir and Estragon wait near a tree for Godot to arrive. They engage in humorous wordplay of dreamscapes and nonsense which has been interpreted as mankind's inexhaustible search for meaning. But Vladimir and Estragon never make any meaning out of their lives and keep waiting, and waiting, and waiting for Godot. The final lines of *Godot* are: "Well, shall we go./Yes, let's go." But they do not move. They remain in place. Waiting, waiting, waiting for Godot just as they were at the beginning of the play.

You see the circular structure at work in *Godot* because the structure offers the audience a sense of futility and stasis, which underscores the themes of the play. There is no logical exposition (early in the play) or resolution (at the end of the play). Once the play ends, the characters are in a similar situation to the beginning of the play and the play could, literally, begin again.

By organizing his character's journeys – or, some say, the characters' very active non-journeys – in a circular structure, Beckett uses comic repetition, which keeps us engaged and connected to the characters while creating a piece of art that is reflective of the hopelessness many people felt in Western Europe after World War II (when he was writing the piece).

Writing Exercise

Take the *Little Red Riding Hood* folktale and write the middle version of her journey. Describe in detail what you think her journey through the forest was like – both what you see in the film and what you can imagine. Do not write her entering the forest. Do not write her exiting the forest. Just focus on what her journey could have been within the forest.

Now, read that description aloud to yourself four times in a row. Do not stop. Just read it over and over and over and over again.

Don't think too hard; just underline what words, images, and moments felt the strongest to you or have the most passion or power, even if you don't know why.

What if you pull these moments out and repeat them? What themes emerge? What ideas? What affect does feeling the circular flow of the words have on you?

In circular plays, there tends to be a unique power in repetition that, while the audience does not always consciously understand, they can feel deeply.

Overview

The circular structure emphasizes repeated journeys and events where characters begin and end in the same place.

---

(4) Pattern

In the pattern play structure, you repeat the same pattern of scenes or moments over and over again. Pattern plays are usually about how or why something happens in society over and over again.

For example, playwright Arthur Schnitzler's *La Ronde* is set in 1890s Vienna, and the structure is ten scenes between pairs of lovers.

One of each pair of lovers shows up in the following scene. Then, one of the characters from the first scene also appears in the last scene.

The scenes are comprised of encounters between these characters:

- The Whore and the Soldier;
- The Soldier and the Parlor Maid;
- The Parlor Maid and the Young Gentleman;
- The Young Gentleman and the Young Wife;
- The Young Wife and The Husband;
- The Husband and the Little Miss;
- The Little Miss and the Poet;
- The Poet and the Actress;
- The Actress and the Count; and
- The Count and the Whore.

By narrowing the scope of the play to only seeing those characters in intimate moments, Schnitzler thematically highlights how certain physical needs (like sex) transcend class distinctions. It makes a pointed argument that class boundaries – like who is a poor Soldier and who is a rich Count – are false, created by society to enforce hierarchies of wealth and power, and abused by those in power. The structure underscores the theme that the hierarchy of society is unnatural and meaningless.

Overview

Pattern plays are typically about why things happen in society or how the same thing (usually a bad thing) keeps happening over and over again. The repeated moments of action usually build to a clear theme.

(5) Ritual

Whether you attend a Catholic Mass, a Kathak dance, or a performance of *Romeo & Juliet* – rituals and theatre are about making meaning. Contemporary theatre is rooted in ritual performance.

In the U.S., we often think of the ancient Greeks as the origin of theatre. However, ritual and performance were tied together long before the Greeks.

Playwright Amir Al-Azraki of *The Widow* says:

> Some Iraqi scholars, such as Fawzi Rashid, argue that the origins of theatre can be traced back to Mesopotamian culture, predating Greek theatrical traditions. Rashid posits that early ritualistic performances during Mesopotamian festivals, like the Akitu Festival, laid the groundwork for theatrical practices. These performances were diverse, with comedic enactments presented in circular designs during major celebrations and tragic performances staged in designs representing the underworld during the fall. For instance, the performance of Inanna's descent into the underworld is categorized as a tragedy and staged in a setting resembling the underworld. . . . Supporting this theory, Khama'il Shakir Al-Janabi has examined linguistic evidence, identifying Babylonian and Sumerian terms related to theatre, such as "melulu" (play), "mummillu/mummiltu" (actor/actress) and "eina dudu" (the one who speaks to the audience). These linguistic traces are interpreted as evidence of a rich and established theatrical tradition in ancient Mesopotamian societies.[1]

There is documentation of ritual performances occurring around the world from ancient times to the present day.

The terms "ritual" or "ritual performance" are often associated with the rituals or theatre of the past. Today, playwrights use the term "ritual structure" to communicate the inclusion of ritual elements into contemporary plays.

For example, playwright Aleshea Harris' *What to Send Up When It Goes Down* uses a ritual structure. The play shares scenes touching on police brutality, microaggressions, and racial resentment, and audience members participate in the scenes with actions like stepping forward if they've had a certain experience. This is like sacred rituals where you step forward, step back, kneel, or bend at certain moments – marking those moments as important or transformative.

The play's ritual structure demands the audiences fully engage with the moment and, through that engagement, find new meaning, understanding, and connection within themselves and as a community.

In addition to physical participation, other elements of ritual you might encounter within a ritual structure include moments of quiet contemplation, moments of interaction with an object, or moments of making individual choices that shape the collective experience. Sometimes, we think of art as individual forms – separated into categories like "dance," "music," "ritual," or "theatre." While individual pieces of art might fit into the parameters of a single category, they might also incorporate elements from many categories. In ritual structures, we see elements lifted directly from a ritualistic experience and clearly integrated into a play.

Artists and academics debate exactly how to define the terms "ritual," "ritual performance," and "ritual structure." They also debate where you draw the lines between the terms – exactly when does an action move from "ritual" to "ritual performance" to "ritual structure." So, you might read different arguments on this topic. However, what's important for you to know right now is that today's theatre is rooted in ancient rituals and that playwrights still use elements of ritual in their work today.

Overview

Ritual structure borrows elements from existing rituals to amplify the meaning and understanding of the piece.

Group Exercise

Think of a ritual that you have experienced in your life. What were the most meaningful moments of the ritual to you?

Discuss moments you found meaningful and the possible root of the meaning for you; were you connecting with ancestors or finding hope in a belief?

The moments that you find meaningful in your experience with personal rituals might also be elements you use in your plays.

Shifting Structures

Once you learn different structures, you can shift and change them to meet the needs of your play. Here is just one example:

In *Fefu and Her Friends,* playwright María Irene Fornés mixes elements of well-made and episodic structures.

Set in 1935, *Fefu* tells the story of socialite Fefu and seven of her friends who spend the day rehearsing a show for charity. Each of the women is struggling – either privately or publicly – with social conventions which restrict their freedom.

The first scene is a well-made play opening where the women gather in Fefu's country house. It gives us insight into each character, gives us an exposition of their lives, and begins to give us an idea of the social conventions they are struggling with.

Then, the play is split into four scenes that run concurrently and that repeat. Audience members walk around, witnessing the scenes in whichever order they choose. The order in which the audience members see the scenes influences how they think the story plays out (for example, it informs who they think did what to whom).

This unique use of the episodic structure allows the audience to engage with different nuances of the character's struggles while also propelling us through the story. It also operates like the world of high society in which the women live – the audience experiences the moments in different orders and at different times, which changes their view of what happens, much like hearing rumors in the culture determined how the women were seen in the world.

In the final scene of the play, the women reunite in one room (and the audience reunites into one audience), and there is a well-made conclusion to the piece where the different plot lines come together for an explosive climax. Then, much like an episodic play, the play ends without a denouement – there is no wrapping up of the drama. The audience is left to fit together the final pieces of the episodic puzzle.

The audience leaves the performance having experienced a compelling piece of theatre while also debating about the play's characters, actions, and situations depending upon how they experienced the play.

By combining structures, Fornés creates a unique structure that is theatrically compelling, supports the journey of her characters, and underscores the themes of the play.

Plays can also use a structure and combine it with a popular theatrical movement or theatrical idea of their time period. Here is just one example:

In *Mother Courage and Her Children* by playwright Bertolt Brecht, he mixes elements of the episodic structure with elements of the epic theatre movement of the early to mid-20th century. In epic theatre, no effort is made to hide the mechanical workings of the show; for example, sets are rearranged in full view of the audience, and the placement of equipment that is usually hidden, like lights, is in view of the audience. Epic theatre is interested in forcing people to see the world as it is. Brecht combined the episodic structure and elements of the epic theatre movement in *Mother Courage and Her Children.*

Mother Courage is set in 17th-century Europe during the Thirty Years' War. Mother Courage and her children – who die throughout the play – travel through the war in a cart containing provisions that they sell to soldiers and peasants alike. The episodic scenes portray a powerful moment of their journey, and then time jumps to another powerful moment in their journey. Scenes are set years apart, but all take place at some point during the Thirty Years' War.

To this structure, they add elements of the epic, so that the inner workings of the set, lights, and other production elements are seen by the audience.

The company of *Mother Courage* combined an episodic journey through a devastating war with elements of epic theatre to create a structure for their show that told a harrowing story while consistently reminding the audience: this is not just entertainment; this is really what is going to happen if we don't find peaceful ways to live together in the world, and what are you going to do about it?

Both Fornés and Brecht are considered experimental or avant-garde playwrights, which means that they used structure and other theatrical elements in rare and surprising ways that deviated from mainstream theatre of their time.

Playwrights learn from and influence one another by how they structure their plays, even if they never meet.

For example, in *Ruined* by Lynn Nottage, you can see how a playwright takes the ideas of an experimental playwright – in this case, Brecht – and uses them to tell a more traditionally well-made play.

Ruined is set in war-torn Congo and tells the story of a group of women working at a bar who have been raped (therefore, deemed "ruined" by their communities) and exiled. While Nottage employs well-made play structure, she was influenced by how Brecht told the story of *Mother Courage.* She was inspired by his Mother character, and in *Ruined,* we follow her character, Mama Nadi, who is a shrewd businesswoman trying to survive in a war-torn region. Mama Nadi's children are the "ruined" women who work for her.

Playwrights influence each other's work in many ways – including borrowing elements of structure, character, and story.

Overview

Elements of different structures, or organizing principles can be used separately or in combination with one another. Playwrights often reach across generations – learning from one another through their text even when they never actually meet. They borrow and build on what they learn in their own work. This is one reason it is important for playwrights to read and see as much theatre as they can.

Resources
Student Favorites

The plays listed here were some of my students' favorites for illustrating the lessons in this chapter. In workshops, we read scenes from each of these plays and then discuss the different approaches to structure. For homework, each student selects one play to read in full and writes a long scene or short play in the style of that structure.

- Well-made: *Ruined* by Lynn Nottage (Theatre Communications Group)
- Well-made with Direct Address: *The Elaborate Entrance of Chad Deity* by Kristofer Diaz (Concord Theatricals)
- Musical Fugue: *Eliot, A Soldier's Fugue* by Quiara Alegría Hudes (Theatre Communications Group)
- Circular: *The Most Spectacularly Lamentable Trial of Miz Martha Washington* by James Ijames (Dramatists Play Service)

- Pattern: *Mother Play* by Paula Vogel (Concord Theatricals)
- Monologues and Physical Movement: *For Colored Girls Who Have Considered Suicide/When the Rainbow Is Enuf* by Ntozake Shange (Scribner)
- Well-made with a Twist: *The Nether* by Jennifer Haley (Northwestern University Press)
- Experimental: *We're Gonna Die* by Young Jean Lee (Script: Theatre Communications Group. Album: youngjeanlee.org/work/were-gonna-die/)
- Post-Modern Episodic: *Woman Laughing Alone with Salad* by Sheila Callaghan (Concord Theatricals)
- Ritual: *What to Send Up When It Goes down* by Aleshea Harris (Concord Theatricals)

Additional Resource

- *Doodles from the Margins: Three Plays* by Hansol Jung: In this text, Jung literally "doodles in the margins" of her own scripts, showing you her creative thought process as she wrote the plays. (Tripwire Harlot Press, 2022)

Discussed in Chapter

- *Cinderella* (Disney film, 1950)
- *Fefu and Her Friends* by María Irene Fornés (PAJ Publications)
- *The Widow* by Amir Al-Azraki (Contemporary Plays from Iraq/Methuen)
- *La Ronde* by Arthur Schnitzler (Methuen Drama)

- *Little Red Riding Hood* based on a folktale by Valentina and Zinaida Semyonovna Brumberg (1937 short film/youtu.be/xb2vD2ovqE8?si=5rZi-WRreI B8ssQo)
- *Machinal* by Sophie Treadwell (Nick Hern Books)
- *Monster at the End of This Book* by Jon Stone, illustrated by Mike Smollin (Random House)
- *Mother Courage and Her Children* by Bertolt Brecht (Methuen)
- *Romeo and Juliet* by William Shakespeare (Folger Library/Online)
- *Waiting for Godot* by Samuel Beckett (Grove Press)

Note

1   Published with permission of playwright.

18

Other Notes on Structure

What follows are a few more tools to help you chart the structure of your play.

Outlines(-ish)

Playwrights use structure and structure-adjacent activities to organize their writing process. Here are just a few ways they do so:

- Playwrights choose the structure for their play in advance, then outline based on what needs to happen for that structure.
- Playwrights make a bullet-pointed list of everything they think is going to happen.
- Playwrights write out a narrative (like a short story).
- Playwrights write a first draft, then sort through their writing to see what stories, characters, and themes they are interested in pursuing for the next draft. They select a structure and then begin outlining that structure using the material they've generated in the first draft.

- Playwrights write, pause in the middle of the process, and take stock of where they are and what they need to do, like Fahmy described earlier in the book.

A playwright's process might also shift because the ideas for a play come to them in a new way or their life circumstances change. Never be afraid to try out a new practice or process; it might be exactly what you need in that moment (or in the future).

For example, for my dark comedy *The Terrible Girls*, about three women working in a deserted truck stop, I was writing the first scene, and then the rest of the story came to me in one flash. I immediately knew the story and the structure. But when I was writing my Sci-Fi play *Click*, I alternated between writing scenes and doing research because the play was extrapolating from a scientific idea. I'd also had children, and so I had less time to write. So, I outlined the play in detail and broke the outline down into short scenes. Then, I focused on writing each scene during nap time so I wasn't interrupted.

How your life looks in the moment that you're writing often shapes the process you use to write your play, so don't be afraid to shift processes when necessary to get your writing done.

There is no right or wrong way to write. Just write. If you become overwhelmed by the options, simply sit down and let the ideas flow in whatever shape they take. You can figure out how to turn them into a play later. Capture the ideas as they come to you.

Writing Exercise

Since the well-made play structure is so popular, here is an outlining exercise called a Story Paragraph that will help you outline your well-made play. Thinking about your story of your characters, fill in the blanks:

(title) is the story of (protagonist) who wants (want).
However, (antagonist) keeps getting in the way by (what the antagonist does). After (complication), (complication), and

(complication), then (main character) finally (dramatic action) and realizes that (realization). This does/does not change how they move forward in the world because: _____. This change is usually related to your theme. The themes of the play could be: _____.

When writing this paragraph, many other ideas, like specific plot points or character moments, might arise. Write those down on a separate sheet of paper. They can help you create a detailed outline in the future.

Overview

As you write more, you'll learn how your brain dumps, sorts, and organizes information – and you'll figure out how you need to write your play. For now, do what feels best for you. The most important thing is that you write.

Realistic and Non-Realistic Choices

Sometimes, the structure of your play will be connected to whether you are presenting your play world as realistic, non-realistic, or a mix of both. You can make realistic and non-realistic choices in any structure.

In realistic plays, life often unfolds in ways that we are familiar with, like we might go to school on weekdays or the sun rises in the morning and sets in the evening.

For example, in the realistic play *Last Summer at Bluefish Cove* by playwright Jane Chambers, the action occurs in the beach community of Bluefish Cove. A straight woman accidentally ends up at Bluefish Cove after leaving her husband and befriends a group of lesbians on vacation. The lesbians take her in, and she becomes a part of the community.

Each of the characters in the community is struggling to make a large, realistic decision in life: to leave their husband, to re-open a business, and such. Due to the realistic nature of the setting and the character's struggles, Chambers wrote the piece using the well-made structure with a realistic tone.

In non-realistic plays, life unfolds in unexpected ways, often with heightened theatricality.

For example, playwright Adrienne Kennedy's *Funnyhouse of a Negro* is non-realistic because it takes a deep dive into the mind of Sarah, a young woman who is experiencing an internal struggle with her racial identity.

To show this struggle, Kennedy transforms the stage into a manifestation of Sarah's mind and uses historical figures to represent Sarah's mixed Black and white ancestry. These choices – a non-realistic, fluidly structured play – give the audience unique access to Sarah's internal struggles and an experience of what she is feeling internally. It also gives us insight into the complexity of identity which is part of the theme of the play.

Both Kennedy's and Chamber's choices were right for the story the playwright wanted to tell and the themes they wanted to highlight. Their structures are the organizing principles that help them share their ideas in a way that the audience can perceive them, and their realistic or non-realistic choices.

Overview

Choices like whether or not your play is realistic or non-realistic connect with your intent for the play. It can also influence your choice of structure.

Fun Fact: The Ghost Light

Many theaters leave a light onstage, often a bare bulb, so the stage is never completely dark. In theatre lore, this allows the ghosts who haunt the theatre to perform onstage when the theatre is closed. Therefore, they will not feel the need to perform when the actual show is running and interrupt the performance.

Aristotle's Poetics

Aristotle's *Poetics* is considered the foundational text of Western Theater.[1] It was written around 335 BCE and is one of the earliest surviving works of Ancient Greek dramatic theory. Although it was lost to the Western world for hundreds of years, it gained prominence in the 1400–1500s through an Arabic version translated into Latin by scholar Ibn Rushd.[2]

There are still many questions surrounding the text and Aristotle's original intent, but what's important for us right now is:

(1) Knowing that it has had a significant impact on playwriting.
(2) Learning how to use the tools it provides to strengthen our plays.

Poetics offers Aristotle's thoughts on tragic play and its six formative elements. Those elements are:

- *Plot*: Usually considered the most important of the six elements of tragedy. Plot means the arrangement of the incidents that we see within the piece. (This is not to be confused with the story of the piece, which is all the incidents of the plot plus what happens on and off stage to the characters.)
- *Character:* The people presented in the play, their traits, and motivations.
- *Thought:* Thought comprises both the rational processes through which characters come to decisions, as represented in the drama, as well as the values put forward in the form of maxims and proverbs.

- *Diction*: The medium of language or expression through which the characters reveal their thoughts and feelings.
- *Song*: A major medium of language or expression that "should" be included in tragedy. This could mean literal singing or the overall musicality and rhythm of the play itself.
- *Spectacle*: The theatrical effect presented on the stage, including special effects, props, set, movement, and other spectacular happenings. This includes song, dance, masks, and more.

While you are writing and revising, you can use this list of elements as reminders of what can make a theatrical experience compelling. You can even select one of Aristotle's elements and add, or emphasize, them in your play. How does that change the work? What other ways of thinking about the work does it inspire for you, and how can that move you forward?

Group Exercise

Write a scene set at a local fair that incorporates all of Aristotle's Elements. Write for at least half an hour. Really give yourself the opportunity to explore what the elements have to offer your storytelling.

Share your scene with your group. Can they spot all of the elements? If so, great! If not, think about how you could have used the element(s) that your friend did not see more fully to make the scene more dynamic.

Playwrights use the elements to think about how to structure their plays.

Most playwrights have abandoned Aristotle's more restrictive ideas on what makes a good tragedy, but a list of his three Unities follows. (He thought a good tragic play should encompass all three of these Unities.) If you get stuck, consider applying one of these rules to your own script to help you think about your play in new and different ways:

- Unity of Time: All action in the play occurs within 24 hours.
- Unity of Place: All action occurs in one location.
- Unity of Action: There is only one main plot, no sub-plots.

Ask yourself questions like: "If you compress your story so everything occurs within a 24-hour period, what happens?" These types of questions can help you think about how you structure your story in different ways. Then, you can choose the structure that best supports your intent for the play.

If you are curious about *The Poetics,* I encourage you to read the entire document. It is still widely available, and many playwrights find it useful as a jumping-off point for how they think about writing plays.

Overview

Poetics is a tool to help us understand the foundations of theatrical storytelling, but it should not restrict creative imagination.

Catharsis

Aristotle used the term catharsis* in *Poetics* to describe a feeling of relief and release people felt at the end of a theatrical performance. This idea of release can inform the structure of your play.

Catharsis is from the Ancient Greek word *katharsis,* which means purification or cleansing. After this purification, the goal is for the person to have an emotional release and feel renewed or restored emotionally.

It's like singing along to punk music or dancing along to a favorite song to relieve feelings of anger or stress. By engaging with a work of art you can purge yourself of those emotions without hurting yourself or someone else. Sometimes, you even discover more about yourself through sharing this moment with a work of art.

Aristotle used the play *Oedipus the King* by the playwright Sophocles (420s BC) as an example of catharsis:

- Oedipus is the King of Thebes, and Thebes is suffering from a plague; his people are dying.
- He sends his brother to consult the Oracle at Delphi. The Oracle has the gift of prophecy; she can explain the mystical underpinnings of the world.
- The Oracle says Thebes is suffering for religious reasons – because the murderer of the former king, Laius, was never caught and punished, so the Gods are angry.
- Jocasta the Queen – who was first married to Laius and is now married to Oedipus – tries to comfort Oedipus.

- Next, Oedipus decides to go on a quest to find and punish the murderer. Through his journey, he discovers that he actually killed Laius – the former king – by mistake in a roadside accident. Oedipus also discovers that he was Laius's long lost son who had been abandoned as an infant. Oedipus is the killer that he seeks! And not only is he the murderer, but he killed his own biological father and married his biological mother, Jocasta.
- At the end of the play, Jocasta commits suicide offstage. Oedipus blinds himself in despair and begs his brother to look after his daughters so they can have a better life than their father.

The play takes us on a clear journey through misfortune, terror, heartbreak, and surprise. The audience is engaged by the story and characters – experiencing the ups and downs of their journey with them but from the safe space of the imagination. So that, by the end of the play, there is a buildup and release of emotions – a purging of emotions – that is cathartic.

The specific emotions that Aristotle highlights as cathartic releases in *Oedipus* are pity and fear. We pity Oedipus because we deeply connect with being human, imperfect, and often in situations beyond our control. We hate to see suffering. We fear that terrible things beyond our control will happen to us. By experiencing Oedipus' story along with him, we move through an emotional journey and reach a catharsis, a release of pity and fear.

There are many different points of view on whether a play must have catharsis, what catharsis looks like, and how it is defined in a theatrical context. For now, just know that catharsis can be a part of your play if you wish, and you can use it as a tool to help write your play.

Overview

Catharsis is an emotional release for the audience.

Who Is Your Audience?

Your structure can also be influenced by the audience you are writing for; do you envision them being adults or babies? Are you creating a play with a community

---

If you have trouble sitting down to write, commit to writing seven pages a week; it can be one page per day or multiple pages on set days.

If you write, more writing will come. If you wait for the Muse to inspire you, you might never get a word down on paper.

When I had small children, I'd stay up one night a week for an extra two hours and just write whatever came to mind (characters, scenes, moments). Sometimes, this writing ended up onstage, but most of it did not. However, it kept my writing skills sharp for when I was ready to sit down and write a full-length play again.

that is to be performed within that community? If you don't know who your audience is early in the process, that's fine. But, some playwrights want to write for specific types of audiences, and that can shape their work.

For example, there are plays for teens and young adults, often co-created by students and professional artists. Playwrights David Lee White and Kate Brennan of *ALiEN8* specialize in these projects:

> In creating our works, we've been able to sit in rehearsal rooms with high school and college actors and make them full collaborators. In the process, they learn about the creation of new work. They learn how to express themselves, how to tackle complex situations, how to work as a team, and more. As wonderful as it is for a young actor to step into a show that's already developed and has been around for decades, it's equally important for them to see how it all begins and to have their voices be at the center of creation. It shapes how we approach creating the work as well as the form and content of the work itself.[3]

Overview

If you know the audience that you wish to write for, then it might shape your work.

First Drafts

Remember: First drafts are just that. First. They are the immediate spillage from your brain. Don't judge yourself too harshly. Don't be too critical. You're going to revise the pages anyway, so just get the ideas in your head out onto the page – no matter how shapeless and weird they might look. Having a first draft gives you something to work with that moves your process forward.

Playwright Connor McPherson of *The Weir* says:

> The best plays come in a flash. An image, a feeling, and that's it. You know these ideas because they are the undeniable ones that won't let go. They pull you in and compel you to start scribbling notes. If you are a playwright and you have one of these on the go, you know you have a responsibility. To what? Something that doesn't exist? But the good ideas feel like they do exist. They're just beyond view, and you're trying to capture them with glimpses that may or may not be accurate. Many playwrights I've talked with agree that the best moments are often those tentative notes when the ghosts first present themselves in your mind. They are so insubstantial yet bear their complete mysterious history within. This is when playwriting is at its most private and, paradoxically, when the play is at its most beautiful. The more real you make it, the less magic it retains. You are aware of this but what can you do? You keep going. Always writing at the very edge of your limitations. And your limitations are not necessarily a bad thing. Your limitations are in fact what give you your unique voice. But it's hard to view your limitations in a warm light when

> ## Check-In
>
> At this point, move on to writing your first full draft of your play. It will be big and messy, and that's okay. Whatever your first draft is, it is what it needs to be. Just write.

you've just read over your work and it makes you embarrassed.

The truth is nobody really knows how to write a good play. You just do your best to avoid writing a bad one. The rest falls to fate.[4]

Resources
Student Favorites

The plays listed here were some of my students' favorites for illustrating the lessons in this chapter.

- Monologue Play: *Pumpgirl* by Abbie Spallen (Faber and Faber)
- Realist Play: *A Doll's House* by Henrik Ibsen (Project Gutenberg/eBook #2542)
- Greek Tragedy: *An Oresteia: Agamemnon by Aiskhylos; Elektra by Sophokles; Orestes by Euripides* by Anne Carson (Farrar, Straus, and Giroux)
- Flexible Structure: *Woyzeck* by Georg Büchner (Nick Hern) (This play can be easily reorganized and reassembled as an educational experiment.)
- A Cycle of Plays: *Ufot Family Cycle: Sojourners* (Dramatists Play Service), *The Grove, Runboyrun*

(New York Theatre Workshop Bookshop), *Her Portmanteau* (Dramatists Play Service), *Kufre n' Quay, The Ceremony, Lifted, in Old Age* (New York Theatre Workshop Bookshop), and *Adiaha and Clora Snatch Joy* by Mfoniso Udofia

Additional Resource

- *Decentered Playwriting,* edited by Carolyn M. Dunn, Eric Micha Holmes, and Les Hunter, shares playwriting structures and practices that are not as broadly taught as traditional Western storytelling structures and creative traditions. (Routledge, 2023)

Discussed in Chapter

- *ALiEN8* by Kate Brennan and David Lee White (YouthPLAYS)
- *Cinderella* (Disney film, 1950)
- *Click* by Jacqueline Goldfinger (Theatrical Rights Worldwide)
- *Funnyhouse of a Negro* by Adrienne Kennedy (Concord Theatricals)
- *Last Summer at Bluefish Cove* by Jane Chambers (out of print but can be found in libraries)
- *Oedipus the King* by Sophocles (translated by Angie Varakis and Don Taylor/Methuen Drama: Student Editions)
- *The Terrible Girls* by Jacqueline Goldfinger (Playscripts)
- *The Weir* by Connor McPherson (Nick Hern Books)

Notes

1 The Project Gutenberg Ebook of *Poetics* by Aristotle, https://www.gutenberg.org/files/1974/1974-h/1974-h.htm
2 *A History of Literary Criticism: From Plato to the Present* by M.A.R. Habib, Wiley-Blackwell Publisher, 2007.
3 Printed with permission of playwrights, 2024.
4 *Conor McPherson: A Flash, an Image, a Feeling – the Mysterious Art of Playwriting*, Nick Hern Books, April 2013, https://nickhernbooksblog.com/2013/04/23/conor-mcpherson-a-flash-an-image-a-feeling-the-mysterious-art-of-playwriting/

19

Play Designations

What follows is a list of popular designations and example plays to read.

Adaptations

Adaptations are plays based on pre-existing materials. Learn more about adaptation and translation in the book I co-authored with Allison Horsley, *Writing Adaptations and Translations for the Stage*.

College/University

These plays are written for college age (18+ audiences) and older. These plays often feature characters in their 20s and include pop culture elements. Read: *In Love and Warcraft* by Madhuri Shekar (Concord Theatricals).

Contemporary Fairy Tale

These plays are often adaptations of classic fairy tales. However, there are plays that borrow the elements of traditional fairy tales and infuse them into contemporary stories. Read: *The Betrothed* by Dipika Guha (Concord Theatricals).

Documentary Theatre

These plays incorporate real-life interviews, and other close studies of real events, to document the world in a theatrical context. Read: *The Laramie Project and The Laramie Project: Ten Years Later* by Tectonic Theatre Project (Vintage).

Horror

Plays that theatricalize horror elements. Read: *Zombie: The American* by Robert O'Hara (Theatrical Rights Worldwide).

Interactive Plays

These plays offer the audience an opportunity to chime in and determine the direction of the show. Read: *Too Much Light Makes the Baby Go Blind* by the Neo-Futurists (*225 Plays By the New York Neo-Futurists from Too Much Light Makes the Baby Go Blind*/Hope and Nonthings Press).

Online

Playwrights are beginning to create work that lives both onstage in real life and online. Read: *She Kills Monsters* (online edition) by Qui Nguyen (Concord Theatricals).

Sci-Fi

Science Fiction plays use Sci-Fi elements – from literal robots to setting the play in a distant future – to tell a story in a theatrical way. Read: *R.U.R.* by Karel Čapek, translated by Claudia Novack-Jones (Penguin Classics).

TYA Family Plays

"TYA" stands for Theatre for Young Audiences. TYA shows are often performed by people of all ages. Read: *Jabari Dreams of Freedom* (ages 8+) by Nambi E. Kelley.

Community Engaged Theatre

These are plays that work with a community to create a script and performance that speaks directly to questions and concerns within that community. For example, in California's Cornerstone Theater Company's *Venice Storytellers 2021*, over 24 artists and neighborhood residents collaborated to create short pieces based on stories from the Venice Community around the themes of history, home, and art.

Overview

There are many different types of plays. There is no limit to how you can use your knowledge of playwriting to create work.

Resource
Additional Resource

- *Rarities and Wonders* by Phillip Howze is an array of actions, disclosures, marvels, and meanderings that asks, "What is a Play?" and explores how and why we make theatre. (Tripwire Harlot Press, 2022)

20

Short Plays

Short plays are a popular and unique form that uses the same elements of a full-length play but in different ways.

What is a Short Play?

Short plays range from 1–50 minutes in the United States. The most popular form of short play in the U.S. are 10-Minute Plays. These are plays that last about 10-minutes (sometimes 8–12 minutes) and include elements of a full-length play, like character, conflict, and structure. However, those elements are shorter in duration; for example, a character might face one conflict in a short play as opposed to multiple conflicts in a full-length play.

Director and Dramaturg Beth Greenberg says that

> Every play and opera has a 'right-size'; the 'right-size' is the length of the piece. Sometimes, you have enough story to fill a satisfying three-hour epic. Sometimes, you have enough to fill a satisfying 10-minute play. One goal of the artist is to discover the 'right-size' of their play, so the length of the play adds to the power of the piece. If a play is too

   DOI: 10.4324/9781003505310-22

long, or too short for their story, then the play can feel awkward and unwieldy. Also, the 'right-size' cast will naturally support the ideal length.[1]

In a classroom, writing short plays can also be a great way to practice different craft skills, especially for emerging playwrights. In my Playwriting 101 workshops, we write 10-minute plays and 30-minute plays. The goal is not to write the best short play ever – but if that happens, great! The goal is to practice using different elements of craft. For example, do you have a strong conflict? If not, how can you strengthen it? Are your characters clearly delineated? Are they going after something? It is easy to isolate and practice craft skills in a shorter play.

Overview

Short plays miniaturize the elements of longer plays, which changes how those elements are used.

Play Versus Skit or Comedy Sketch

While I enjoy skits and sketch comedy, short plays are a slightly different form. Where skits and sketch comedy typically center on one joke, or a series of related jokes, plays focus on characters and their journeys.

Of course, plays can have jokes, while skits and sketches can have great characters. The difference is that the play focuses more on characters and dramatic arcs* than skits and sketches, while skits and sketches focus more on the jokes than the characters and dramatic arcs. The difference between the forms is a matter of what you focus on writing within the piece.

For example, in a play about two people on a first date, the characters might make funny remarks to charm one another, but the play centers on the dramatic question, "Will they or won't they become a couple by the end of the play?" The comedy is an integral part of the play, but it is not the core of the play.

But in a comedy skit or sketch about a first date, there will be a long stream of entertaining jokes which we enjoy but probably won't really care if the couple gets together or not.

If you are wondering if your short play is a play, skit, or comedy sketch, ask yourself: does my play have compelling characters and an engaging dramatic question? If you have both, then it is probably a play.

Also, it's important to know that some artists do not differentiate between a play, skit, or sketch. They call all those types of work short plays.

Writing Exercise

The "who/why/now" monologue is a great writing exercise for short plays because it drops you quickly into the character's backstory and world.

A "who/why/now" monologue is an imaginary prologue to the play; it's what we'd hear before the play began to help us understand how the character got into this situation.

Each of the following steps in the monologue writing process can be as many, or as few, words as you wish. The goal is just to learn a bit about the life trajectory and goals of your character.

(1) Step One "Who": Write about "who" the character is; usually about where they come from, perhaps a significant moment in their life that has influenced them greatly. This can be as simple as "I was born in ___ and my young life was like _____."

(2) Step Two "Why": Explore the "why" of the character, usually one or two specific important events that influenced who they became.

(3) Step Three "Now": Explore the "now" of the character, who they are today, and what their values and goals in life are. It also tells us what is happening in this present moment right before the play begins.

A "who/why/now" monologue doesn't usually appear in my final play. However, it tells me enough about a character, their history, and their situation to begin writing my short play.

Here's an example of a "now/what/why" monologue from You Tong's *Black and White Donkeys* (17th century) where an elderly woman who excelled at sword fighting and now trains young women in sword fighting opens the play with this monologue:

Step One, the "Who":

Long ago when I was the maiden of Zhao, I excelled at the art of sword fighting. Goujian, the King of Yue, heard about my skill and summoned me to his throne.

Step Two, the "Why":

Along the way, I came upon an old man who called himself "Mr. Yuan" and asked to put his skill against mine. He then plucked a stalk of bamboo from the forest's edge. I took up the tip, and he grasped the base of the stem to try and stab me. I then struck him with my staff. He flew up into the tree and changed into a white gibbon, then fled. From that tie onward, I was enlightened and then went on to live as a recluse; I've been here in the Zhongnan Mountains for round about a thousand years. Now, I'm already shorn of hair as a nun, and I've already gone through the rituals of initiation into pure karma. Why is it then that I still pass on this art of sword fighting that I practice to later generations? It is simply because this world continues to abound with disloyal ministers and thieving sons, wild husbands and unfaithful wives. Not only is it difficult to rein them in with the laws of the state, but even Buddha coming to the world can't save them. I simply need this dagger in my sack, and the deed is done in a split second-this is for the great use of putting the Way into action on behalf of Heaven and protecting the people on behalf of the state. Over the years, I've instructed no fewer than 100 disciples.

Step Three, the "Now":

At present I have two girl disciples. One is Li the Twelfth of Linying, and the other is Jing the Thirteenth of Suzhou. Both are ten years old. They have mastered the art of breath control and no longer need to eat. They can run along cliffs just like flying birds. Yesterday, when I was in Weibo Circuit, I happened to see the daughter of the great General Nic Feng whose childhood name is Yinniang. She is also about ten years old, and quick with a gentle grace to her, so I asked the general whether I could take her along with me. He flew into a rage and berated me, but I just smiled and said, "Even if you lock her inside an iron box, I will surely still take her away." And that night, I did indeed take her away and brought her here to this place. The girl has immortal bones in her body and was not frightened in the least. Why don't I call her to come out and teach her some tricks with the sword? Yinniang, where are you?[2]

Now, select a character you've created for a short play and write a "who/why/now" monologue.

After writing it, think about: What did you learn about this character? What was expected? What was unexpected? What is the launching point for your story? Now, you're ready to either continue pre-writing or jump into writing a first draft of a short play.

Overview

Skits or comedy sketches focus on the joke. Plays focus on compelling characters and engaging dramatic questions.

Miniaturizing Play Structure

A short play can have any play structure, i.e., organizing principle. The structure is compressed to fit the given time frame.

In addition, short plays jump right into the middle of the action. There is little to no "set-up" of the situation.

For example, a full-length play about a teacher and her students disagreeing over class reading would probably begin with the set-up of the characters and situation. But, in a short play, you'd probably begin with the teacher and students in the classroom arguing over which book they should read. In the short play, we jump into the middle of the action.

The endings of short plays are different from the endings of full-length plays as well. In a full-length play, a character might make a major choice or have a significant realization, and then we see the results of that choice or realization. We see the outcome of those final moments. But in short plays, we typically just see the character's final major action – for example, making a choice, having a realization, or going back to the status quo – then the play ends. We typically do not see the consequences of their final action on other characters or their world.

Overview

Short play structures are compressed to fit the shorter time frame of the piece.

Short Play Productions

Short plays are produced in a show that contains a number of short plays that equal the length of a full-length play. Producers often select plays that explore a similar theme (e.g., lost love). Short play producers tend to select plays that work well together as works of art but also that can be easily produced side-by-side. So, they might select plays that can share a set or don't need any set at all. Most short play festivals do not feature large casts, so make sure you really need every character that's onstage in your play.

Overview

Short plays have different production considerations, which are useful to know about so that you can write plays that are easier to produce if you wish to do so.

> ## Writing through Movement to End Writer's Block by playwright C. Quintana of Scissoring
>
> So often we forget that our writing lives in the body. Sometimes in order to unlock work on the page, it's worthwhile to invite the energy in through movement.
>
> I encourage you to think about what in your life or art (or both!) is upsetting you, enraging you, making you sad beyond belief, and take a favorite up-tempo song – for example, at least a minute Celia Cruz's *Yo Viviré* (*I Will Survive*) – to really dance, shake it out, *let it all go*. You can even move directly from your seat, but I encourage you to rise from your chair, move across the space, if you are able, and *really* give in to the music! Remember, this is not about "dancing" or any ability – it's about shaking ideas loose, literally!
>
> Now, as soon as the song is over, take pen to paper and write for *at least* ten minutes. Try to be free as you write, don't anticipate what's to come, let the spirit of the song and the movement stir you.

Resources
Student Favorites

The plays listed here were some of my students' favorite short plays.

- Plays that are 15-Minutes or Less in *TRW Presents: Short Plays Volume 2* (Theatrical Rights World-wide), which span the gamut from laugh-out-loud comedy to serious drama.

- *Fake News* by Doug Wright
- *As Slimy as Young Snails* by Arlene Hutton
- *Disney & Fujikawa* by Lloyd Suh
- *G.O.A.T.* by Ngozi Anyanwu
- *La Traviata* by Lisa D'Amour
- *Locked and Loaded. Can I Help You?* by David Ives
- *Swastika* by Elaine Romero
- *Twilight Visit* by MJ Kaufman

- Longer One Acts:
- *Brother/Sister Plays* by Terell Alvin McCraney (Theatre Communications Group)
- *Sister Mary Ignatius Explains It All For You* by Christopher Durang (Grove Press)

Additional Resource

- Advice for Playwrights by Simon Stephens, who works with playwrights of all experience levels: youtu.be/Yl94vFSywwk?si=w8LvXSTgFizErJ-a (Paines Plough)

Discussed in Chapter

- *Black and White Donkeys* by You Tong (*A Topsy-Turvy World: Short Plays and Farces from the Ming and Qing Dynasties*/Columbia University Press)
- *Scissoring* by C. Quintana (Dramatists Play Service)

Notes

1 Printed with permission of Beth Greenberg, 2024.
2 From *A Topsy-Turvy World: Short Plays and Farces from the Ming and Qing Dynasties* by Wilt L. Idema, Wai-Yee Li, and Stephen H. West, Copyright 2023, Columbia University Press.

21
Feedback and Collaboration

Congratulations, you've written a play!

Collaboration

Great collaborators are there for you both when you succeed and when you fail. The strongest artists and artistic collaborators both celebrate your successes and understand how painful and difficult it is to try your hardest and still fail to achieve your artistic goals. So, they embrace failure as a necessary part of growth. They are rigorous with one another's work but respectful of the person who created it.

There are many collaborative artists involved in these processes, including Director*, Dramaturg*, Designer*, Actor/Performer*, Producer*, Stage Manager*, Choreographer*, Fight Choreographer*, Intimacy Director*, and Crew*.

Collaborators should work as partners toward each other's development, not as adversaries or detractors. If someone causes you actual harm and claims it's for the good of your art, then walk away from them. Their need to inflict harm – in the form of racism, sexism, or in other ways – is a problem within them, not a way to help you.

Art is not suffering. Suffering is suffering. There are moments in everyone's life when they suffer, and some people deal with that suffering by making art. Some of that art is great, some of it is not. Using art as a coping skill is a life-affirming choice because you are choosing to make something rather than let suffering destroy you.

But art isn't great because the artist suffers; it's great because the artist encounters something in themselves or in their world and chooses to investigate it; they ask questions like, Why? Or, What If? Or, Could It Be? Then, they share that investigation with the world.

You should be rigorous in your art-making, and sometimes that rigor requires asking difficult questions about yourself and the world, questions that uncover difficult truths or emotions for you – but rigor does not equal deep harm, especially when it comes from someone who is supposed to be your advocate.

Overview

Be open to feedback about your work, but you do not need to experience racism, sexism, or other harmful behaviors as you receive feedback. Throughout the process, you will have many types of collaborators.

Feedback

Learning how to give and receive feedback is an art form.

Thoughts on collaboration from playwright Rachel Lynett of Apologies to Lorraine Hansberry (You Too August Wilson)

Collaboration in playmaking and theatre is so incredibly vital to the art form. For my process, I tend to write what I call a "skeleton" draft and then immediately send it out to work with collaborators. I don't believe I can have a true first draft until after I've sat with actors and theatremakers talking about the bones of the piece. Because of this, I think collaboration has to happen way before the first rehearsal of a production.

Collaboration for me is vital because theatre is meant to be performed, both seen and heard. A playwright knows how a character lives on the page but actors know how a character lives in the body. A playwright knows how the world they're attempting to build live in the multiverse, but directors know how the world can exist on stage, wherever that stage may be and designers know how to bring that vision to life. We all depend on each other to create a performance so we should collaborate as soon as words hit the page.

Theatre is a collectivist model and as we're trying to find a way to evolve and reinvigorate the art form, we must remove individualism from the process.

Outside of that very heady space, collaborating is what makes theatre fun. It's exciting to see an actor find something in a character you didn't know where was there or a director choose a color that lightens (or darkens) the world of the play. We call them plays because that's exactly what we should be doing: playing. And no one should have to play alone if they don't want to.

As you grow as a writer and have more experiences with collaborators, you'll learn who to take a note from – and when to take it. For example, if someone doesn't like the end of your play, then the note might be, "I don't find the end compelling." However, that note could mean many things. For example, it could mean:

- The person does not understand the ending.
- You need to change the ending.
- The ending does work, but you've overwritten or underwritten it.
- The ending does work, but an earlier moment in the play is not working. You need to change that moment so the ending moment makes sense.

As you have more experience receiving and giving feedback, you'll begin to figure out what feedback is on-target for you and your work and what is not useful.

An important way to know whether feedback is useful is to consider your intent for the piece. The intent is what you want the piece to do and/or to be. Knowing your intent will help you decide which feedback is useful.

For example, if we are writing *Little Red Riding Hood* and our intent is to emphasize the importance of family bonds, then we might revise the story to include more scenes between Little Red Riding Hood and Grandma.

But if we are writing *Little Red Riding Hood* and our intent is to emphasize the horror, then we might write longer scenes with the Wolf in the forest and at Grandmother's house.

Both versions of the story can be interesting; how we write and revise it depends on our intent for the piece. Also, our intent for the piece may change as we go through the learning process of revision, and the play tells us more about what it wants to be.

In feedback sessions, craft questions that speak directly to your intent for the play. Here are a few examples:

- What did you think the play was about?
- Who did you think the main character was?
- Which character did you connect with the most? Why?
- Which character interested you the least? Why?
- What are the moments that made you lean forward/ engaged you most?
- Where were the moments you were unsure of what was happening in the story?
- In scene three, were you surprised when the mother was released from prison?

When you begin working with actors, directors, and other intimate collaborators, each will have their own ideas about your work – which is good! It means that you'll receive feedback from different points of view.

After you've received feedback, take time to reflect on the feedback itself and who was offering it. For example, I find that actors tend to offer the most useful feedback on the emotional lives of their characters. Professor and acting teacher Sara Shockley Thompson cites noted actor and teacher Uta Hagen:

> In her book *Respect for Acting*, Hagen says that the first job for an actor involves discovering the character being portrayed. Not only must actors learn who they will be onstage but must also consider the character as a well-rounded human being, making certain to avoid clichéd generalities. 'Every detail of place, objects, relationships to others, my main character's needs, my immediate needs, and obstacles must be made particular. Nothing should be allowed to remain general,' wrote Hagen. Such priorities mirror those of the playwright who must create characters with specific qualities, so that they may be fully fleshed out, Hagen says to actors, "You must see what you have to see in order to tell the story or see it so that it doesn't distort the story."

While I consider feedback from everyone in the process, I pay special attention to actors when they are discussing their character's internal life.

When you're receiving a lot of feedback, it can be useful to consider who the feedback is coming from, in addition to the feedback itself. Your intent, or goals, for the piece might be different than someone else's, so they might give you feedback based on what they want to see in the piece (rather than what you want the piece to express). To them, their notes make your play "better." But, really, the feedback just makes your play different – and different in a way that is more interesting to that person but not to you.

For example, Playwright Charles Mee of *Big Love* describes his intent this way:

> My own work begins with the belief that human beings are, as Aristotle said, social creatures — that we are the product not just of psychology, but also of history and of culture, that we often express our histories and cultures in ways even we are not conscious of, that the culture speaks through us, grabs us and throws us to the ground, cries out, silences us.
>
> I don't write "political plays" in the usual sense of the term; but I write out of the belief that we are creatures of our history and culture and gender and politics — that our beings and actions arise from that complex of influences and forces and motivations, that our lives are more rich and complex than can be reduced to a single source of human motivation.
>
> So I try in my work to get past traditional forms of psychological realism, to bring into the frame of the plays material from history, philosophy, insanity, inattention, distractedness, judicial theory, sudden violent passion, lyricism, the National Enquirer, nostalgia, longing, aspiration, literary criticism, anguish, confusion, inability.

I like plays that are not too neat, too finished, too presentable. My plays are broken, jagged, filled with sharp edges, filled with things that take sudden turns, career into each other, smash up, veer off in sickening turns. That feels good to me. It feels like my life. It feels like the world.

And then I like to put this—with some sense of struggle remaining—into a classical form, a Greek form, or a beautiful dance theatre piece, or some other effort at civilization.[1]

His interests are clear. So, if he is assigned a director who only wants to direct politically realistic plays then the director might give Mee feedback that would change Mee's plays to be more realistic and politically polemical. This would cause conflict between playwright and director because the director is not respecting Mee's intention for his work.

As you write more plays and work with a wide range of collaborators, you'll discover your personal interests, point of view, and intent for your work. This knowledge will help you find collaborators who support and strengthen your work.

Thoughts on Feedback and Revision from playwright Madeline Sayet of Where We Belong

Anyone who directs or adapts the classics knows you can remove or add a line to change the meaning of an entire scene. Any play's cultural context can be altered by adjusting whose lens is centered and how a piece begins or ends. Who we identify with or don't matters and what kinds of people you take feedback from will affect this.

Revision is where you find the depth and possibility you were seeking, but it can also be the thing that kills the heart of a play if you forget yourself in the process. I respond well to lots of dialogue in process – so I always begin with a 20 minute mini draft – the trunk of the tree – and then once I hear it read the idea grows and the branches and roots extend out and in. I very rarely use Aristotelian structure, and am more interested in building ecosystems of characters, and fluid time. When I rewrite I always go back to the beginning of the text, because the rhythm of the journey and how it builds is very important to me. (This takes too much time, I aspire to not have to do this).

But, I think it's really important that you know what your values are as a writer and the values of a piece, story, character, question who you are engaging with. Otherwise the voices in the story can get muddled by the voices of the people outside of it.

Why are you writing it? What are you trying to investigate? What audience do you care most about? Even when you feel forced to take a note, don't compromise what matters – there are ways to take a note in a circuitous direction if you don't agree with its initial intent.[2]

I recommend that you begin your feedback process using the existing model of Liz Lerman's Critical Response Process. As you learn more about your own creative process, then you can continue to use this model or create one of your own.

Through the supportive structure of Lerman's four core steps, the process offers playwrights an active role in the critique of their own work and empowers them to move forward. An overview of these steps:

- Step 1: Statements of Meaning
  - Facilitator asks responders to state what was meaningful, evocative, interesting, exciting, and/or striking in the work they have just witnessed.
  - For example, "When I saw the child slap her mother, I was moved and engaged."

- Step 2: Artist as Questioner
  - The artist asks questions about the work. In answering, responders stay on topic with the question and may express opinions in direct response to the artist's questions.
  - For example, if a playwright wants to know if the reason behind an action is clear, they might ask the question, "Why do you think the child slapped the mother?" This will tell the playwright what the responders perceive as the reason behind the slap – and that perception may or may not be what the playwright intends. If their response is not what the playwright intends, then this might be a place in the script to focus on during revision.

- Step 3: Neutral Questions
  - Responders ask neutral questions about the work, and the artist responds. Questions are neutral when they do not have an opinion couched in them.
  - For example, neutral questions are like, "I'm curious to hear more about your intent behind having the child slap the mother." These questions help the artist investigate their play, which often leads to a process of revision, as they know more about their play and how it is being perceived.
- Step 4: Opinion Time
  - Responders state opinions, subject to permission from the artist. The usual form is "I have an opinion about _____; would you like to hear it?" The artist has the option to say no.
  - For example, "I have an opinion about the child slapping the mother; would you like to hear it?"
- After Step 4, I often ask playwrights what their next steps are or what they think they will tackle first in their rewrite. This helps them focus on how to move forward rather than getting bogged down by all the feedback, which can be overwhelming, especially for new writers.

You can read about the Lerman process in-depth in the book *Critical Response Process: a method for getting useful feedback on anything you make, from dance to dessert.*[3]

Overview

Giving and taking feedback is an art form. As you mature as a writer, you will discover the most useful ways for you to receive feedback. You should also be mindful of how you give feedback and make sure that the type of feedback you are giving is the type of feedback the artist needs.

Resources
Additional Resources

- *Directing New Plays: Tools for Art and Collaboration* by Evan Cabnet. Focus on Chapters 1–3 which discusses the role of the director and how a direction can approach a text. (Methuen Drama, 2024)

- *The Process of Dramaturgy* by Scott R. Irelan, Anne Fletcher, and Julie Felise Dubiner. Focus on Chapter 5 on New Play Dramaturgy. (Hackett Publishing, 2010)
- *Theatre Begins Here* podcast from the Playwrights Center interviews a host of theatre artists. You can submit questions to be answered by podcast guests. (pwcenter.org/membership-podcast-theater-begins-here/)

Discussed in Chapter

- *Apologies to Lorraine Hansberry (You Too August Wilson)* by Rachel Lynett (Yale Press)
- *Critical Response Process: A Method for Getting Useful Feedback on Anything You Make, from Dance to Dessert* by Liz Lerman and John Borstel (lizlerman.com/critical-response-process/)
- *Respect for Acting* by Uta Hagen (Jossey-Bass)
- *The (re)making project* by Charles Mee (charlesmee.org)
- *Where We Belong* by Madeline Sayet (Methuen)

Notes

1 From Charles Mee website, https://www.charlesmee.org/charles-mee.shtml, 2024.
2 Printed with permission of the playwright, 2024.
3 From Liz Lerman's website, https://lizlerman.com/critical-response-process/, 2024.

22

Revision

Revision is a fluid process. It can take a month or ten years. At some point, you must let the play go, know you've learned a lot, and it's time to apply what you've learned to a new play.

Revision

The most important thing to remember about the revision process is that . . . it's only on paper.

It's only on paper. You can do anything on paper. You can take chances. You can write a monologue and discard it, then pick it up again two drafts later. Be fearless in revision because it's only on paper. There are no risks, only rewards. If you decide you don't like the changes one day, you just return to the older draft. (Make sure to save a draft as a separate file every day, so you can always have copies of previous material, in case you want to use it.)

The second most important thing to remember about the revision is that . . . it's a learning process.

Revision is peeling the onion of your story, excavating layer by layer until you've written the strongest play that you can write. Then let it go.

DOI: 10.4324/9781003505310-24

Revision writing can be more difficult than writing the original draft. When you're writing the first draft, the world is your oyster. You can throw in everything you want – your favorite dragon, the kid next door, and your kitchen sink.

But when you revise, you take a deeper look at the art and craft of the piece. Much like life, every decision you make as you revise narrows other decisions you can make in the future (see Chapter 10: Play World, *Rules of the World*). Luckily, in art, we can always go back and change our choices, giving us new options and unlimited permutations of the play.

For my first draft, I include everything that I want in the play. It is messy, inconsistent, and full of contradictions. My second draft is weaker and less interesting than the first draft because I'm still trying to find my characters and story. I make missteps along the way (like removing the wrong monologue or writing superfluous scenes). However, what I've learned through writing multiple plays is that all my tangential meanderings in draft two lead to a stronger draft three. Meandering is just part of my process.

Playwrights have different revision practices.

For example, some playwrights begin revision from the blank page again; they re-read the script, receive feedback from trusted collaborators, allow ideas to percolate, and then begin writing again from page one. While other playwrights select moments they feel are most true to the play, then they revise those moments and write new pages between those moments to connect them.

Playwright Virginia Grise of *Blu* says, "I have never arrived anywhere in a straight line, so I don't know how to tell a story that way."[1] She is not alone. As you write and revise more work, you'll have a better understanding of what process fits your needs.

At some point in the revision process, playwrights have a moment where it feels like the play begins to speak for itself. When it comes to that point in revision, playwright Jessica Huang of *Song of Northwoods* said, "Doubt yourself. Trust the play."[2]

It's like having a child; at first, you guide them, but as they grow, they begin to guide themselves, make their own decisions, and become their own person. When the characters begin speaking in their own voices – even if they say things you don't expect – listen to them. Write it all down. It is a great sign. It means that you've given them enough depth, nuance, and specificity to become their own people.

Overview

At the end of the metaphorical day, a work of art is never done. All we can do is try our best and release it into the world to find its own life.

On Revision and Community from theatre artist Leila Ghaznavi, creator of Silken Veils, *and who originated the character Yasmine for the Sesame Street Workshop:*

There are a lot of adages about the revision process "Writing is rewriting" and "Kill your babies" jump to mind. My personal favorite is "Revision is remodeling, not dusting the furniture."

All of them summon to my mind the image of a writer hunched at a desk surrounded by crumbled coffee-stained pages. In a fevered haze, the writer scribbles the same few words over and over until each letter and punctuation mark is perfectly placed on the page. Across the arts, we glorify the vision of the tortured creator who strives alone in darkness with only a solitary candle flame – lit by a spark of inspiration – to guide them.

I'd like to offer something different. "Revision is an act of community." I know, it's not nearly as pithy. But my experiences in ensemble theater quickly taught me that there is greater depth of problem-solving prowess in a group than can ever be found in the limitations of one individual's solitary mind. When you start the revision process never hesitate to call upon your community for help.

Community comes in all shapes and sizes. It can be a trusted reader, an editor, a dramaturg, an ensemble, a test audience, or a random passerby at a coffee shop that idly asks what you were working on as you doodle on a napkin. This doesn't mean that you must take every suggestion or critique given to you. Your job is to be a sieve, sifting through the information provided, seizing with glee the dustings of gold that will gild your final product, while discarding the lumps of rocks that don't serve you. Even someone's "bad ideas" have their usefulness. They confirm for you where you *don't* want to go thus illuminating the paths for where you *do* want to go because it's in the opposite direction of *that*.

All of us stand on the shoulders of our community. Shakespeare, Frida Kahlo, T.S. Eliot, Arthur Miller, there is not artist you can name that didn't have a community of some shape or size to support them. So do the work, put in the hours at your desk, but remember "Art" is the pinnacle that is remembered by history, but all great art sits on the bedrock of the community that helped build it.[3]

Revision and Relationship: Speaking to the Conscious, the Unconscious, and the Subconscious

Art speaks to our conscious minds as well as our unconscious and subconscious:

- Our conscious is the part of our minds that is aware of our surroundings and believes it understands the reasons for our responses and choices in life.
- Our unconscious is the deep recesses of our past and memories that live residually in our minds,

bodies, and spirits that we don't consciously remember but still affect us.

- Our subconscious is our automatic actions and reactions that we don't notice unless we focus our attention on them and dig down into why we made those choices.

Moments in our plays will resonate with audiences consciously, unconsciously, and subconsciously, for example:

- The audience knows why a moment is powerful to them.
- The audience doesn't know why a moment is powerful to them but is still compelled by the moment. This often happens with "the specific becomes the universal" because the core truth of the moment onstage speaks to the core truth within themselves – even if they don't know that they hold that core truth within themselves.
- The audience reacts negatively to a moment – even if it is well done – because it makes them uncomfortable on a visceral level, and they can't separate that visceral response from how well the moment of art is crafted.

Revision can make a play more compelling, enlightening, and illuminating. It speaks to the core relationship of theatre – the relationship between artist and audience. There are many layers to this relationship – some of which you will predict, some of which you will not. But as the play moves through development, workshop, and production – you will see their responses emerge. You do not have to revise to meet audience expectations. However, it can be useful to see an audience's reaction so you can make a more informed decision about how you want to shape the play.

Overview

Being rigorous and purposeful with revision will make your play resonate with your audience on multiple levels. These resonances bond you and your audiences together in a sacred relationship that transcends us as individuals and even the work itself.

Revision Tactics

Playwright Steven Dietz of *Bloomsday* offers these thoughts on approaching revision:

> What we call "revision" is the remarkable gift of not having to get everything right the first time. We don't have to revise our plays; we get to revise our plays. We are not due praise for this act. Revision is not a virtue; it is a tactic. It is the ongoing opportunity to make the events told/depicted onstage more electric, intentional and impactful. The word revision literally means 'to see again.' We have the rare chance in the theatre (alone among all of literature and the performing arts) to see our play again – not

only throughout its development, but even after it has been viewed by audiences. What a gift.

A few tools and tactics for your consideration:

There are not two writers inside you. There is not a wild-and-free generative writer who magically spins out the initial draft, followed by a cold-and-critical pragmatic writer who pounds out the revisions. You are both of these writers – in every moment, throughout the life of your play. Critique is essentially choice, and choice is the root of creativity. Let your critical voice be alive as you create; let your creative voice be alive as you revise. Scrutinize as you generate; explore as you refine.

Ask actionable questions about your play – both of yourself, and in every feedback session you lead. An actionable question is one that, when answered, gives you a tangible thing to address. These are questions based on the things you control (content, structure, delivery), not the things you don't control (relate-ability, like-ability, produce-ability). You are seeking reportage and not reflection. Actionable Questions: "What was the moment you knew Diane was going to leave?" "At what point did the power shift in the friendship between Ron and Bill?" "What's the thing you thought Angie would never do?" Non-Actionable Questions: "Did it work?" "Could you follow it?" "What really 'popped' for you?" Your revision will only be as strong as the actionable questions you ask of your play.

Active engagement with your play means that everything is alive and in play – at all times. No part of your work is off limits. Remember that your play is not 'flawed'; it is young. As such, it seeks nourishment. Trust that it is tough. Trust that it doesn't need your protection; it needs your attention. The only way to kill a play is to coddle it.

Be the last one done with your play. When everyone agrees it is 'ready,' give it one more pass and find that change/cut you had overlooked. (There will be one. There always is.) Will this make a difference to the play? Certainly. But it will make a bigger difference in you. Every time we rigorously attend to our craft, we deepen our craft. Endeavor to make this productive scrutiny habitual.

Final word comes from a gardener friend of mine: "We prune the trees we love."

Dietz's parting thoughts remind us of the classic advice the playwright Aeschylus of *The Oresteia*, who said: "From a small seed a mighty trunk may grow."[4]

My parting thoughts: Be conscientious and take time with what you bring into the world. It has feathers; it will fly.

Overview

Revision is a learning process. Through that process, you'll discover the intent of your play (if you haven't so far), and this allows you to write towards your intent.

---

*Writer's Block Prompt from playwright
Sharon Bridgforth of* bull-jean:

Thinking about writer's block always moves me to think about the creative process.

Instead of worrying with moving blocks, I encourage you to ask yourself, "What is my creative process?" What moves, motivates, informs your writing? What are the constants that you notice that happen in concert with your writing flow? For real. It doesn't have to make linear sense.

For instance, for me, my process starts with a feeling. Something deep and unnamable (at first). I find music that matches the feeling and I put that music on repeat.

I engage in conversations and seek information (via research, conversations and sometimes travel) that vibrates with the feeling.

I follow joy, curiosity and passion.

I pay rigorous attention to what is.

And eventually the work moves through me in ways that I can name, know, apply craft and move towards collaboration with.

Notice what your body is telling you.
Honor what is swirling within and around you.
Feed yourself with Inspiration.
Consider the truth that you are never not writing.
Ask yourself what your creative process is.
Nurture and tend that.

> ## Check-In
>
> If writing a play as you move through this book, move into revision. Break legs!

Resources

Additional Resources

- *36 Assumptions about Playwriting* by Jose Rivera (tellinghumans.org/jose-rivera-s-36-assumptions)
- Pixar animation studio is a storytelling powerhouse, and they've shared their *22 Rules of Storytelling*. They offer you some ideas about how to revise your play (mes153.commons.gc.cuny.edu/files/2018/08/Pixars-22-Rules-of-Storytelling.pdf, 2018)

Discussed in Chapter

- *Bloomsday* by Steven Dietz (Dramatists Play Service)
- *Blu* by Virginia Grise (Yale Press)
- *bull-jean* & *dem/dey back* performance/novels by Sharon Bridgforth (53rd Street Press)
- *The Oresteia* by Aeschylus
- *Silken Veils* by Leila Ghaznavi (panteaproductions.com)
- *Song of Northwoods* by Jessica Huang (Audible)

Notes

1   Printed with permission of the playwright, 2024.
2   *Tips on Revision*, Playwrights Center Blog, 2019.
3   Printed with permission of the playwright, 2024.
4   "Aeschylus Quotes," *BrainyQuote.com*. BrainyMedia Inc, September 28, 2020, https://www.brainyquote.com/quotes/aeschylus_398833

23

The Business of Playwriting

Playwriting as a career is a mix of art, craft, and business. Right now, while you are learning, I recommend ignoring the industry and writing what you want and need to write. You can figure out the business part in the future.

Art and Business

There are two important aspects of my life as a playwright:

(1) The Creative Aspect.
(2) The Business Aspect.

The Creative Aspect is my favorite. It's writing and revising plays. It's being in developmental workshops and full productions. It's reading and watching as much as I can to deepen myself as a person and an artist.

The Business Aspect is awkward for me. It encompasses submitting plays, networking at events, and creating marketing materials. It is confronting the reality that producers must work within a vast matrix of constraints – including budget, location, donor interests, and mission statements – when they select shows for production.

 DOI: 10.4324/9781003505310-25

And that, no matter how much they love my play, they might not be able to produce it, if my play does not fit within that matrix.

I encourage you to keep these two aspects of life as a playwright – the art and the industry – in separate parts of your brain and create your own metrics for success. That way, you can enjoy the work for its own sake, no matter what is happening in the industry.

Unfortunately, in the U.S., very few playwrights make a living writing plays. Playwrights have other day jobs – including writing for TV and film, teaching, or an office job – that pay their bills. So, you can be a well-established playwright and still not make a living from it.

Many playwrights write for the meaning it brings to their lives, whether or not they make money from it. Playwright Adam Szymkowicz of *Letters to a Young Playwright* writes:

> We make art because art feeds us. I think most people think the point of art is to share something with the world, to make people laugh or cry or think. To rewire someone's brain. That's valid. But I think that's actually the secondary effect of art. The main thing art does is for the artist – to make their life better. Everyone is different, but for me, my mental health is better on a day when I've written something. It helps my mood somehow, the act of expressing myself. And if I can get into a flow state where I'm writing but I'm no longer aware of time, that always centers and grounds me. What I'm

trying to say is that art-making, like exercise or yoga or getting a massage, is a form of self-care. If we have souls, making art nourishes our souls. And it's not really anything exclusive or magical. Anyone can benefit from making art, and you don't have to be any good at it in order for it to make your life better. Sometimes it's as simple as doodling on a page or writing an idea down in a notebook or whatever your version of this is: Strumming a guitar. Arranging rocks on a beach. Because also art is lots of different things. Sometimes enriching your soul by making art is a slog. Sitting down to write is not always fun, but the more you do it, the easier it will become to slip into the flow state.[1]

Personally, writing plays is my way of understanding the world. In daily life, we are busy and often jump from moment to moment without much reflection. But on-stage? We are forced to slow down and breathe. We see, we hear, we feel, we vibrate, we cleanse, we rally, and we rail. We have time to examine and reflect. To laugh at ourselves. To find humanity in others (even those we loathe and despise). When writing a play, I spill all of my fears, my hopes, my confusions onto the page. I focus my energy on understanding what's happening so that I can create a cohesive story that brings meaning to my life and, hopefully, to the lives of others. My playwriting is a sanctuary where joy is plentiful, conversations are nuanced and deep, and we are all valued for our innate humanity. We are not necessarily at peace, but we do have hope for a better tomorrow.

There is no one "right" way to become a playwright. Some playwrights study in school, others undertake fellowships and mentorships, yet others become playwrights in their own time on their own independent paths. Playwright J.T. Rogers of *Corruption* says:

> I didn't go to writing school, I didn't have any mentors as a writer, so when I started out, I was just sort of aping what I saw around me. Much of it is dear to me, a few were quite successful, but they were before that moment you need as an artist – whatever your discipline – when you figure out, "Oh, why don't I write about what *I'm* interested in, and not what everyone else is telling me I should write about." And so, it was a bit of an "A-ha" moment for me, years ago. You figure out, if this is what I'm really interested in as a person, then maybe that's what you should write your plays about. It sounds so obvious! But I'm not the first – and I won't be the last – playwright to have that all-incredible-yet-banal thunderbolt hit them.[2]

Regardless of where your journey leads you – see theatre, see art, talk about art, talk about life, find a community where you can experiment/experience/thrive. This will fill your life with joy, beauty, and complexity. The act of creation – of making something and sharing in something that someone else has made – is an act of hope and connection that enriches all our lives.

Overview

Write because you want to write – whatever that reason is, is the right reason. What's important is that it's a meaningful process for you.

Playwright R. Eric Thomas of Mrs. Harrison on Development and Production

Making a play is a collaborative effort at every step and that includes figuring out how you're going to get your play read, developed, and considered. It's common to want to simply send off a script and hope for the best. I've done that a lot. But it's more productive, I've found, to cultivate relationships with people who can get to know your voice, your interests, your killable darlings, and your working style far before a word gets on the page. Keep up with directors whose work you like, see theater when you travel and drop lines to the Artistic Directors and Literary Managers who programmed it, slide professionally into the DMs of designers whose work blew you away. You don't need to go in with an ask; you need to go in with curiosity and a desire to be part of a larger ecosystem. Those relationships can turn into partnerships. Or friendships. People may think of you for commissions or development opportunities. Directors or designers with established relationships at other theaters may pitch your plays because they want to work on them, thereby allowing you a chance to get into a new space. Though writing–fingers on a keyboard–can often seem solitary, the business of writing is all about relationships. And the best relationships aren't transactional. Getting your work seen, read, and produced is also about seeing the work of others and getting to know the people that made it.[3]

Opportunities

There are typically four types of industry opportunities you may wish to pursue: Residency, Development, Production, and Publication:

- Residency: A Residency gives you time, space, and resources to create a new work or strengthen an existing one. For example, you might stay at a special cottage in the wilderness and have meals provided so you can write.
- Development: This is a workshop, reading, or other method through which you strengthen your play. It gives you a chance to hear the play read in the community with other artists and sometimes also with the public so that you can begin to understand how it might translate from the page onto the stage.
- Production: This is a public sharing of the work with production elements (i.e., sound, costumes, props). Usually, the playwright works with all of their collaborators during this process.
- Publication: Publishing a script for reading by a wider audience. Usually, the playwright works with the publisher during this process. Publishers usually want to publish a script after it has been produced.

Playwright Craig Pospisil of Journey to the Poles of Inaccessibility *on New Play Publishing*

The business side of playwriting might not seem like something to consider when you're writing, but knowledge of the business can be like good notes from a dramaturge. I've spent my entire career as a playwright also working at play publishing and licensing companies, and the business side of the industry is something I use like an editor looking over my shoulder.

There are stark differences between what most professional theaters can and want to produce versus what school groups are looking for – both in terms of cast size and content. Professional theaters want to keep their costs down, so they look for small cast plays, but schools want to involve as many students as possible. I'm not advocating you contort your play to try and thread that needle but keeping those production realities in mind can be something of a stress test. Does your play need that character who's only in one scene? If the answer is "yes," professional theaters may balk at a play that makes them hire extra actors. Do your characters drink or swear a lot? If the answer is "yes," schools may not be able to do the play.

Write the play you want to write it the way the story requires. But know what's necessary and what might not be. Economy of language in your dialogue is important, so be economical in how you approach all the aspects of a play in production.[4]

There are many ways to create and share your work in the industry. Always read the fine print for any opportunity to make sure you fully understand your rights and responsibilities.

Playwright Lisa B. Thompson of Underground *on being an emerging, and evolving, artist*

At the beginning of your career, producers, critics, and funders will refer to you as an emerging writer. A considerable amount of attention is paid to rising theatre artists before their first production, and for good reason. We need fresh and inventive narratives about what it means to be human in this moment. New playwrights also bring hope that this beautiful and fragile ecosystem that we call the theatre will continue to thrive and grow. Once you have a few productions under your belt, and hopefully some successes, you will no longer be considered an emerging writer; you may even be described as mid-career. While the moniker may not apply to you any longer, you will always be an emerging writer. While you're more experienced and may have become accustomed to having your work on stage, you are is constantly changing. This strange, wonderful and oftentimes harrowing world will force you to grow. With grace, fortitude, humility, bravery and luck, a different "you" will emerge. The kinds of stories you tell, the challenges you seek as a dramatist, the producers who find you relevant, and the audiences who respond to your work will continue to emerge right along with this new you. Accept and relish the rejections and the triumphs because they shape the next iteration of you. Embrace your changing self because the world needs every version of you. If you continue to write plays, one day you will recall fondly the productions and artists and collaborators that have blessed your work. Toast yourself and celebrate your emergence. Just don't do celebrate too long because there's still plenty of growing ahead.[5]

Developmental Goals

When you are applying for an opportunity, some organizations will ask you for your Development Goals; this means they want to know what you want to get out of the process.

Often, organizations read your work samples first. Then they read the Development Goals of the work samples that they liked the best. They are trying to assess who is going to use their resources the most wisely.

In general, the four questions that organizations want answered in development goals are:

(1) How does this project, specifically, meet their mission and speak to their audience?
(2) How, specifically, would you use their unique resources?

(3) Why is this project important to develop now?

(4) Can you self-diagnose possible weaknesses in your own work and talk about what you would do to strengthen it?

Sometimes, they will ask for developmental goals with a specific focus. For example, they'll ask, "How does this project fit our definition of hope?" In those cases, make sure to emphasize and/or fully focus on the relationship between your project and their question. Follow their lead.

Here is an example of a development goal:

My goal is to have a draft ready to submit for production after XXX's development process. This play has two (eight-hour) readings scheduled: one this summer in XXX and one early in the fall in XXX (this work has never been seen in your city.). Both readings will focus solely on the text, as there is no time to explore the movement sections of the play. I would love to bring what we learn about the text from those readings into the XXX workshop room. I would use the 20-hour process at XXX to explore the movement sections to make sure the idea of the movement in my head actually works onstage, as well as explore alternative movement options. The movement is especially important in understanding the romantic arc of Abbie and Charles, as well as the reason they react so negatively to having a child, which relates to the theme of the play (not all of us are meant to be parents, and that's okay). A 20-hour workshop will ensure that I enrich the characters and give full reign to the complexity of their experiences, both in text and in movement – as the play intends. The movement and the text are inextricably linked in telling this story, and I want to give each enough time to fully bloom in the submission-ready draft.

Overview

Developmental goals are both about your play and how you will use the organization's tools wisely.

Artistic Statements

Artistic statements are much more fluid than Development Goals. Since most organizations cannot afford to fly you in for an interview, the Artistic Statements give the organization a chance to get to know you as a person, your interests, your influences, your hopes, and your dreams.

The Statements are about getting to know you. Don't be afraid to color outside the lines a bit and get messy. Some statements are formal; some are casual. Some are written in paragraph form, and some in free verse. What you want to do is bring a sense of yourself, your individuality, and your uniqueness to the table.

> *Playwright Dave Osmundsen of* Light Switch *has a guide for writing artistic statements that he's been kind enough to share with us. Some of the questions he lists for you to ask yourself are like the questions I asked you*

to list in our Chapter 1 exercise. Feel free to return to that exercise to give you a jumping off point for Dave's exercise.

Your Artist Statement: The Who, the What, the Why, and the How

Writing an effective Artist Statement can be one of the most daunting tasks for a playwright. Some prefer to let the work speak for itself. Others struggle to comprehensively articulate their artistic intent. After writing several Artist Statements over many years, I've developed a formula for what I feel is encompassed in a strong Artist Statement: The Who, the What, the Why, and the How. An Artist Statement should tell theaters WHO you are, WHAT you write, WHY you write, and HOW you write. The following breakdown is a series of questions that can serve as guidelines for your Artist Statement.

The Who

- Who am I?
- Who are my characters?
- Who is my audience?
- Who are my ancestors (theatre artists, writers, historic figures)?

The What

- What do I write about?
- What inspires me?

- What angers me?
- What keeps me up at night?
- What brings me joy?
- What brings me love?
- What brings me hope?
- What brings me fear?
- What brings me struggle?
- What do I want to accomplish?
- What words inspire your work?
- What words encapsulate your work?
- What does your work look like? Feel like? Taste like? Smell like?

The Why

- Why do I need to write about this?
- Why do I need to tell my story?
- Why do I need others to hear my story?
- Why is this work important?

The How

- How does your work move in the world?
- How does your work explore the themes you want to discuss? Theatrical style, tradition, an aesthetic . . .
- How can your artist statement share this aesthetic?

Two More Artist Statement Crafting Prompts

- Imagine your plays are people. What qualities would they have? What makes you get along with them? How do you struggle with them? Have they been easy or painful to bring into the world? Who else has been involved in their upbringing?

· Draw your work. Visualize it. Then describe it. Don't worry about it making sense.

A Note on Finality

There is no finality with Artist Statements. Like any work-in-progress, we are all "in draft." Your Artist Statement can change, shift, and morph depending on where you are in life, where your values lie, and what influences you as an artist and individual. It might be a good idea to periodically revisit your Artist Statement and, using the above questions as guidelines, revise it accordingly.

One of Dave's Artistic Statements

I was diagnosed with Asperger's Syndrome, a form of Autism Spectrum Disorder, when I was three years old. After years of social skills classes, special education programs, and arranged playdates, I was able to present as allistic. When I tell people I'm Autistic, many of them say "You don't *seem* Autistic!"

Hooray for me?

I struggle with this "accomplishment." While I'm able to pass as allistic very well, my "success" doesn't erase the bullying, depression, suicidal ideation, low self-esteem, hyper-fixations, stims, and pervasive anxiety I lived with (and still do). Due to how ashamed

I was often made to feel about my Autism, it took until my mid-twenties to embrace it and use it as a generator for my art. I may have outgrown most of my Autistic behaviors (highly common for Autistic adults), but I still have to live in an allistic world that, in addition to having impossibly high standards for itself, seems increasingly hopeless from a geo-political standpoint.

Given these circumstances, I often ponder my measure and definition of "success," an interrogation that often spills over into my writing. How is "success" defined differently for Allistic and Autistic folks? Can the Allistic and Autistic communities come to a consensus on what "success" looks and feels like? Is "success" defined by emotional fulfillment? Or perhaps financial stability? Can it only be achieved by passing as allistic in a world not designed for Autistic folks? How much currency does authenticity, or the perception of authenticity, have?

For my part, success is measured by how it's received and discussed by the Autistic community I want to represent. Allistic folks, especially advocates for the Autistic community, are welcome to join. But if my work hits with my fellow Autistics, then I know a play of mine is successful.

My plays are variations on the theme of Autistic folks navigating a world not designed for them and wanting to be loved on their own terms and seen as people rather than symbols of hope. This can be explored through an Autistic person's relationship with their allistic family. It can also be explored through how different

Autistic people respond to ableism. Recently, I've become interested in the Autistic community's relationship to history – who are our ancestors, predecessors, and role models, and how can we learn from a past that didn't have the (appropriate) language to define us, and actively worked to eradicate us. Ultimately, I hope to show the American Theatre that Autism is not a spectrum, but rather a constellation, given the innumerable manifestations and stories behind it – stories that are epic and intimate, tragic and joyous, clean and messy, platonic and romantic, mundane and adventurous.

Like life.[6]

Overview

There is no one way to write an artistic statement. Your artistic statement should be a snapshot of where you are as an artist at this specific moment in time.

Playwright Philip Dawkins[7] of Failure: A Love Story *offers advice on Community Connection*

Make it your goal to work with people, not buildings. Institutions are just bricks. But people, artists, creators . . . these should be your inspiration. If every play you see at a certain theatre has a lighting design that takes your breath away, make it your goal to work with that lighting designer. If it's appropriate, reach out to them, tell them specifically what moves you about their work and why you connect with it. Form a creative relationship with a human. And when the theatre eventually closes to earthquake, bed bug infestation or human bafoonery, you will still have that human relationship. Find the people with whom you want to work, not the real estate you might want to do it in.

Resources
Additional Resources

- *Dramaturgy: The Basics* by Anne M. Hamilton and Walter Byongsok Chon. Focus on Chapter 2 *Reading as a Dramaturg* to get insight into how dramaturgs will be reading and evaluating your scripts for different opportunities and Chapter 5 *Dramaturg as Producer and Innovator* to get insight into producing your plays. (Routledge, 2022)
- *How to Playwright* with Audrey Cefaly is a free online magazine with submission opportunities and more. (audreycefaly.substack.com)
- *Letters to a Young Artist: Straight-up Advice on Making a Life in the Arts-For Actors, Performers, Writers, and Artists of Every Kind* by Anna Deavere Smith. (Anchor Publishing, 2008)

Discussed in Chapter

- *Corruption* by J.T. Rogers (Farrar, Straus and Giroux)

- *Failure: A Love Story* by Philip Dawkins (Playscripts)
- *Journey to the Poles of Inaccessibility* by Craig Pospisil (TRW Plays)
- *Letters to a Young Playwright* by Adam Szymkowicz (Applause/Rowman)
- *Light Switch* by Dave Osmundsen (Broadway Play Publishing)
- *Mrs. Harrison* by R. Eric Thomas (TRW Plays)
- *Underground* by Lisa B. Thompson (*Underground, Monroe, and The Mamalogues: Three Plays*/Northwestern University Press)

Notes

1   *Letters to a Young Playwright,* Applause, 2024
2   J.T. Rogers in Conversation with Timeline Theatre, https://timelinetheatre.com/2019/09/a-conversation-with-j-t-rogers/, 2019
3   Printed with permission of playwright, 2024.
4   Printed with permission of playwright, 2024.
5   Printed with permission of playwright, 2024.
6   Printed with permission of playwright, 2024.
7   Printed with permission of playwright, 2024.

24

Film and Television

Playwriting skills transition well into writing for TV and Film, but it does take a lot of work to understand how to evolve your skills. Below is a short essay about the similarities and differences between writing for stage and screen. Many of my students find the online Masterclass sessions with Aaron Sorkin and Shonda Rhimes very useful. Links to those sessions are listed at the end of the chapter.

Writing for the Screen

Playwright and Screenwriter Jennifer Maisel of *Eight Nights* offers a short overview of the art and business of writing for the screen:

So – you're a playwright who is thinking about writing for film and television. What's the big deal? It's writing, right? Writing is writing.

Well, yes. And no.

And before we even start this conversation, if you think you need a thick skin for writing plays and trying to get them produced, let me tell you, you need an infinitely thicker skin to write for television and film. Yet you still

DOI: 10.4324/9781003505310-26

want to write for film and television, so here's some basic information to get you started.

Writing is Writing, Yes And . . .

So yes, writing is writing, and if you are a writer of plays, there's no reason why you shouldn't be able to expand your craft and skill set to write for film and TV. But you need to understand it's an expansion, it's work, work with potentially more financial reward and it's not for the faint-hearted. And you must, must, must play well with others.

In the broadest of strokes, there are two ways writing for theatre differs from writing for film and TV (which, by the way, also differ from each other).

ONE: What's on the page. People like to say if a film script is wordy and conversational, it's like a play. And that's where they are wrong. If you take a conversation between a couple of characters and plunk it on a stage, it's deadly. Because onstage, dialogue is action. There's a tension between these characters, and it's being expressed verbally. How the language is parsed out, how each character responds, and the silences scripted in are all the music of what we experience as an audience. The words give rise to action. There is a magic in the interplay between what's happening onstage and what's being received, responded to, and returned by the audience. When you write a play, you are often discovering it as you go along; you are writing for yourself, and the structure is determined more organically.

In film and television, there is a proscribed format and structure you must learn. Any executive, agent, director, actor, will most likely stop reading after a page because not using correct format signals that you don't know the vocabulary of film and television and why are they going to waste their time? (Your story may be brilliant, but it will not matter because they're not going to finish it.)

And anything that is shown on a screen, large or small, is missing the essential live-ness of theatre. There is no interplay between the audience and the art that changes the tenor of that particular viewing experience. While a film or television show is edited, polished, and locked.

A production of a play always has the possibility of the element of surprise that can only be experienced in that particular performance. How a play works is contingent upon who the audience is made up of; it changes. How TV/film works? It exists, and nothing about who is seeing it changes what it is.

Script Formatting

You can even see the difference when you look at how a play is formatted versus a film/television script. Dialogue takes priority in a play script and goes margin to margin (traditionally – theatre is more open to an organic layout on the page that reflects what needs to happen on stage), and the stage directions are often minimal.

Action takes priority in a film TV script – the action is written from margin to margin, and the dialogue space is minimized. In screenwriting, we look at a script and value the white space. We want the eyes to be led easily from description to dialogue to description; we are writing to create a visual experience in the reader so they can see it unfold for them, they can be drawn in, and, ultimately, they will think this story reads like something worth backing with millions of dollars to make it real.

Creation and Process

TWO: The other difference – How we go about creation and process.

A play script is, essentially, yours. And if you are fortunate enough to get a production – or multiple productions – they all start with your words, which they cannot change, but the elements of the production will; the actors, the set, the stage, the blocking, the music, the lights. The play starts with your ideas, your words. You will definitely be given feedback along the way, but it is your choice to take it or not.

One way to put this is – in playwriting the collaboration often begins after you've written the script when actors, directors, designers, and dramaturgs bring their talents to the table, which may inspire you to make changes, but they can't mandate them.

In film and television, the collaboration occurs from the idea through writing the script – and often continues without you while it goes into production.

A film or television script also starts with the words you say. Well, not exactly. While you will need to write spec after spec [a speculative screenplay that is not solicited by a producer] to hone your craft and prove again and again you can write, writing for film and television is a lot of . . . not writing for film and television.

The Pitch

In Hollywood, you need to become the master of the pitch. It's actually just as important, if not more, than the actual writing. It's tough because many a playwright isn't really expert or comfortable distilling their story down to the thrilling essential plot points and presenting them in a way that's dynamic and makes whoever is on the receiving say, "I want to make that!"

Often people are great pitchers and not-so-great writers or great writers and not-so-great pitchers. I am a better writer than I am a pitcher. I work my ass off at pitches, I rehearse again and again, I freeze, I shake. I know people who take beta blockers. Whatever works.

And once you've gotten someone to commit to making said pitch into the TV show or film, you will experience a very different process of writing for the screen:

- You will be pitching and outlining extensively if you're writing a film or a pilot.
- You will be listening to feedback every step of the way, often from multiple people, and you need to satisfy those notes at each step. It will be a long time until you get to write, and then, believe me, you will be rewriting based on notes again and again.

- You will have to learn the language of notes and figure out what the producers are really looking for.
- And at some point, the powers that be may decide you've taken it as far you can, and they hire someone else to make it better. And you will have to let go, weep into your snacks, and gear yourself up to start all over again.
- It's important to note that if you are staffed on a television show, you will be breaking story, and often writing by committee. That is a special skill in and of itself and takes a certain kind of person, one who can not only take thoughts and expand upon them but one who doesn't get thwarted by the "no's" and keeps enthusiastically generating ideas while the "no's" slide off you.

So, if, at this point, you are still a playwright who wants to write for film and television, and you are prepared to expand your creative skill set into related yet not-quite-the-same medium and have a drawer of snacks to weep into just in case, now all you have to do is be strong-hearted, thick-skinned, resilient – and start writing.

Overview

Even though you can use playwriting skills to write for film and television, there are significant differences in the art, craft, and industry.

Resources
Student Favorites

The plays listed here were some of my students' favorite plays about working in film and television.

- *Fade* by Tanya Saracho (Concord Theatricals)
  - When Lucia, a Mexican-born novelist, gets her first TV writing job, she feels a bit out of place on the white male-dominated set. Lucia quickly becomes friends with the only other Latino around, whose story finds its way into the TV scripts that Lucia writes.

- *The Farnsworth Invention* by Aaron Sorkin (Concord Theatricals)
  - It's 1929. Two ambitious visionaries race against each other to invent a device called "television."

Additional Resources

- Aaron Sorkin Masterclass in Screenwriting: masterclass.com (Masterclass)
- Shonda Rhimes Masterclass in Writing for Television: masterclass.com (Masterclass)

25

Extra Credit

Always be reading. Always be engaging with art and seeing theatre in all its forms. Even when you encounter work that does not excite you, you can learn from it; ask yourself questions like, "What do I think the artist intended with this piece? How do I see it impacting other audience members?"

Additional Readings

What follows is a list of 25 plays that I include on "extra credit" lists for my students. Students read the play and then write an essay about at least one craft element and how it is used successfully, or, about the history of the play and the playwright.

- Anonymous, *Everyman* (Project Gutenberg/eBook #19481)
- Behn, Aphra, *The Rover* (*The Rover and Other Plays*/Oxford World Classics)
- Calderón, Guillermo, *Kiss* (Concord Theatricals)
- Desleal, Alvaró Menén, Black Light (*A Dozen Orgies: Latin American Plays of the 20th Century*)
- Dring, Lisa, *Sumo* (New Play Exchange)

- Drury, Jackie Sibblies, *Fairview* (Theatre Communications Group)
- Ferrentino, Lindsey, *The Fear of 13* (Nick Hern Books)
- Glaspell, Susan, *Trifles* (Project Gutenberg/eBook #59432)
- Hrotsvitha, *Abraham* (Project Gutenberg/eBook #59770)
- Iizuka, Naomi, *Anon(ymous)* (Playscripts)
- Kane, Sarah, *Blasted* (Methuen/explicit violent content)
- Khoury, Sylvia, *Selling Kabul* (Theatrical Rights Worldwide)
- Mallén, Ana Caro de, *Count Partinuplés* (*Women Playwrights of Early Modern Spain/* Iter Press)
- O'Brien, Dan, *Body of An American* (Concord Theatricals)
- O'Neill, Eugene, *A Moon for the Misbegotten* (Yale Press)
- Ping, Chin Woon, *Details Cannot Body Wants* (*Postcolonial Plays*/Routledge)
- Schiller, Friedrich, *The Robbers* (Project Gutenberg/eBook #6782)
- Shifu, Wang, *The Story of the Western Wing* (University of California Press)
- Sigurjónsson, Jóhann, *Eyvind of the Hills* (Project Gutenberg/eBook #21937)
- Silverman, Jen, *The Moors* (*Three Plays*/Oberon)
- Sutherland, Efua, *The Marriage of Anansewa* (Longman African Classics Series)

- Toossi, Sanaz, *English* (Theatre Communications Group)
- Tremblay, Michel, *The Real World?* (Talonbooks)
- Usigli, Rodolfo, *The Imposter* (Discoveries Series/ Latin American Literary Review Press)
- Yamauchi, Wakako, *And the Soul Shall Dance* (*Songs My Mother Taught Me*/Feminist Press at CUNY)

Resource
Additional Resource

- *Light Fantastic: Adventures in Theatre* by John Lahr is a series of enjoyable essays about popular theatre artists, mostly from the U.S.A. in the 20th century. Focus on reading Part II. (Dial Press, 1996)

Glossary

This list contains definitions of common theatrical terms. The first time you encounter these terms in the book, you will notice they are starred (*).

Actor/Performer: A person who interprets a character and brings them to life on stage.

Antagonist: A character who opposes the protagonist's goals, usually the secondary focus of the play. The antagonist does not need to be "evil" or the "bad guy." There are plenty of antagonists who are well-meaning or act in positive ways but are opposed to the protagonist's goals.

Appropriation: The action of taking something for one's own use, typically without the owner's permission (that something can be physical or cultural).

Arc: How the play and/or character develops from the beginning of the play to the end of the play.

Atmosphere: The overall feeling the play world itself projects.

Beat: Beat has different meanings to different artists. Sometimes, people use the word "beat" to describe a new moment on stage. For example, Beat One is when the character jumps for joy because they think they've won the lottery. Beat Two is the next beat, when they become sad because they realize that they were wrong and have not won the lottery. Other artists use beat to mean a series of moments that are connected. Make sure to clarify with your collaborators what they mean by "beat."

Catharsis: The release or "cleansing" of emotion at the play's end.

Character: The people or animals or inanimate objects made animate – the active beings – in a play.

Choreographer: This collaborator is trained in movement and/or dance. They help create movement sequences safely.

Climax: The point of highest tension in the story when the character makes the biggest decision of the play.

Collaborators: People you work with to develop and produce a show; for example, actors, dramaturgs, directors, designers.

Complications: Obstacles or opportunities that get in the way of your character achieving their goals.

Conflict: A struggle between opposing forces in a play, often characters who are in opposition to one another because they want different things. The conflict may occur within a character as well as between characters. If the conflict occurs within a character, then the playwright finds a way to externalize that conflict on stage.

Crew: A person who ensures that a task gets done, usually during a show (e.g., someone who makes sure the props are in their right place).

Denouement: The end of a "well-made" play where we see how the story turns out.

Designer: A person who imagines and creates an element of the production (e.g., someone who builds props or generates the soundscape).

Development Opportunity: This is a workshop, reading, or other method through which you strengthen your play.

Dialogue: Two or more characters speaking to each other.

Director: A person who interprets a play and creates the version of the play as they see it onstage. They are the driving force of a production.

Downstage: The part of the stage closest to the audience.

Dramatic Action: What the character wants to achieve overall in a scene and/or play.

Dramatic Question: The overarching tension of the play tied to the main character's conflicts.

Dramatic Tension: A state of uncertainty in the play, a tension which often keeps the audience engaged in the performance.

Dramaturg/Director of New Play Development/Literary Manager: A person who supports the artists in their creative process (e.g., creating research packets, offering thoughts on the script) as well as facilitating a deeper understanding of the work for the audience (e.g., leading events surrounding the production). This is a flexible role and varies greatly depending on what the production requires.

Dramaturgy: A study of how a play works and why, as well as how to share that information with both creative collaborators and audience members.

Entrance: When someone or something comes on stage.

Exit: When someone or something leaves the stage.

Exposition: Exposition is the explicit sharing of direct information, usually information that's part of the backstory/what happened in the past or offstage.

Fight Choreographer: This collaborator is trained to help stage fight sequences that are safe for all involved.

Fourth Wall: A theatrical convention where the performers on stage pretend not to see the audience, and the theatrical event continues as if the audience is not there.

Goal: What the character's going after.

Inciting Incident: In a well-made play, it jolts the characters out of their everyday existence and goes on a new journey.

Intention: What a character wants in a scene and why they want it.

Intimacy Director: This collaborator is trained in helping create safe, consensual, and intimate scenes on stage.

Key Moments: Specific moments/memories in your character's histories, lives, and experiences that forever stay with your character and shape the way they think and behave.

Metaphor: A figure of speech that compares two things by describing one thing in terms of another. Metaphors are often used to make ideas more clear or to create vivid imagery. For example, "Mom has a heart of gold."

Meta-Theatrical: These techniques bring the audience's attention to the theatrical devices used in the play. For example, breaking the Fourth Wall is an example of a meta-theatrical device because it says to the audience: "Hey! This is not real! This is theatre!"

Monologue: A story or speech given by a character as part of a scene or alone onstage. A soliloquy is one form of a monologue. In a soliloquy, a character speaks to themselves out loud.

Mood: How the piece makes you, the audience, feel.

Naturalism: A theatrical movement beginning in the 19th century that advocated putting real life – as close as we can to it – on stage. The people, settings, conflicts, and actions should all be grounded in realism – the realities of everyday life. These plays often explore or expose social issues (like food insecurity or racial bias). For example, in Naturalistic play, characters would drink actual water out of cups.

Objective: What the character wants most in the scene, a term primarily used by actors.

Obstacle: What gets in the way of what the character wants.

Pacing: The speed at which the play moves.

Plot: The series of events that we see on stage.

Producer/Artistic Director/Artistic Producer: A person who oversees and pays for the production. They often have a say in the choices made for the production.

Production: This is a public sharing of the work with production elements (i.e., sound, costumes, props).

Protagonist: A character going after something, usually the main focus of the play.

Raising the Stakes: Increase the risk of the actions a character takes.

Realism: A style that tries to give an illusion of reality onstage. For example, in a naturalistic play, characters would drink actual water out of cups. But in a Realistic play, they might pretend to drink water out of cups. Both are meant to represent what is real, just in different ways.

Realization: Usually, it happens at the climax of a play where a character takes lessons they have learned throughout their journey and comes to a new place of understanding of themselves, their world, or a situation.

Rhythm: Slightly different from pacing but often connected to it. While pacing determines how fast or slow the narrative unfolds from moment to moment, rhythm is the overall flow throughout the play.

Rising Action: The character tries to overcome conflicts to reach their ultimate goal.

Scene: A unit of stage time where something happens that the audience can perceive, and that adds meaning to the piece.

Simile: The comparison of one thing with another thing of a different kind. For example, "brave as a lion."

Stage Directions: Instructions in the text of a play that primarily share unspoken physical movement or offer a sense of character emotion or prevailing tone. They can also offer insights into lighting, sound effects, and offer other stage notes.

Stage Left: The left side of the stage from the actor's point of view as they look at the audience.

Stage Manager: A person who keeps the daily schedule on track, facilitates communication within the company, and otherwise supports the artistic and practical needs of the artists.

Stage Right: The right side of the stage from the actor's point of view as they look at the audience.

Stakes: This is what happens if a character fails or succeeds. This fuels the audience's connection to the character because, generally, the audience cares whether the character fails or succeeds.

Status Quo: At the beginning of a well-made play, we see the character's everyday life as it existed before the story began.

Stereotype: A widely held but fixed and oversimplified image or idea of a particular type of person, community, or thing.

Story: The plot, as well as everything surrounding the plot, how the characters feel, unexpected happenings, what happened before the play begins, and what happens offstage.

Subtext: The unspoken or implied meaning behind the words.

Super-Objective: The goal of the character for an entire story, a term primarily used by actors.

Symbol: Refers to the use of an action, object, or name to represent an idea or quality. In theatre, it's often taking an emotion or idea and associating it with a physical object.

Tactics: The different approaches someone tries to get what they want.

Theme: An idea that recurs in or pervades a work of art or literature for emphasis.

Timing: Most frequently refers to the way characters interact. When a character is asked a question, do they reply quickly, pause to think, or shake their head and then leave the stage?

Tone: The way the characters speak and move through the play world which also contributes to the atmosphere.

Transition (and Beat): "Transition" often means moving from one state to the next state in a performative way. For our characters, this can mean a change in state, whether physical, emotional, or psychological; a character going from happy to sad is a transition. For our scenes, we can have scene transitions where we move from one scene to the next. For the music, this might mean going from one song to the next. The important thing to remember is that a transition is active, and the audience experiences it (e.g., sees it or feels a shift in emotion). Sometimes, people use the word "beat" to describe a new moment on stage. In that case, the transition is how we move out of one beat and into another.

Upstage: The side of the stage closest to the back wall; the area at the actor's back when they face the audience.

Appendix A
Saving and Formatting Your Script

An overview of saving scripts and adjusting the script format to your needs.

Saving Documents

Save the play with a new date every day you write, so you have each day's script saved as a separate document.

Overview

Save everything. You might want to return to certain pages in the future.

Formatting Scripts

Plays have a title page with the title of the play and your name and contact information on it. Then comes a page listing the characters, settings, time period, and any additional short production notes. Then comes the actual play.

Now, let's talk about formatting the actual pages of your play. For first drafts, the most important thing is that you write. If you sit down and the words come out in free verse, great! If they come out in an industry format, wonderful! If they come out with large gaps between them, perfection! How you put the words on the page is less important than putting them on the page.

However, when you are submitting work for consideration, it's most important that you read the submission guidelines carefully and use the required format when you apply.

Here are a few different ways that plays can be formatted:

Playwright David Auburn's *Proof* is published in a manuscript format, meaning that publishers use this format for publication.

In *Proof,* Catherine, a young woman, has given up college to return home and take care of her mentally ill math genius father. When he dies, an astounding mathematical proof is discovered on his desk and is thought to be his final work. Then it's revealed that Catherine wrote the proof.

As a play set in contemporary times, featuring characters that speak in generally realistic/everyday ways, setting the play in long lines of dialogue works beautifully. It is an example of the "manuscript format" working for a play text.

Proof formatting looks like this:

CATHERINE: Dialogue Dialogue Dialogue
      (Stage Directions* Stage Directions)
HAL: Dialogue Dialogue Dialogue Dialogue Dialogue Dialogue
   logue
CATHERINE: Dialogue Dialogue
      (Stage Direction Stage Direction)
HAL: Dialogue

The playwright Annie Baker's *The Antipodes* is published with text at different places on the page throughout the entire play.

Since the play is set in a room where storytellers are brainstorming, creating, and refining stories, the movement of the words on the page is flowing, overlapping, and evolving. These line settings help us understand how the play should feel when it's on the stage. It also highlights one of the themes – which is the slippery, always evolving nature of storytelling itself.

The Antipodes looks like this:

She writes her stage directions across the page.

SARAH
Dialogue Dialogue Dialogue Dialogue Dialogue
SANDY
Dialogue Dialogue Dialogue Dialogue Dialogue Dialogue
   Dialogue Dialogue Dialogue

> *She writes her stage directions across the page.*
>
> ADAM   JOSH   DAVE
>
> Dialogue   Dialogue Dialogue   Dialogue
>
> Dialogue   Dialogue
>
>   Dialogue
>
>   SARAH
>
> Dialogue Dialogue Dialogue Dialogue Dialogue Dialogue
>   Dialogue Dialogue Dialogue

In *Andy Warhol in Iran,* celebrity artist Andy Warhol traveled to Iran to take Polaroid pictures of the Shah's wife. This imagined experience of an encounter with a young Iranian radical is a heightened play about art, revolution, and discovering a world beyond yourself.

Playwright Brent Askari writes Andy Warhol's dialogue in short poetic lines with no punctuation for the first 12 pages of the play. During this time, Andy directly addresses the audience and discusses his views on art and the world. The choice to use short poetic lines gives us a sense of floating above reality.

When Farhad, the other character, arrives, Askari erects a Fourth Wall between the performers and the audience, so it becomes a play where the characters do not acknowledge the audience. The dialogue becomes more realistic and rooted in reality. At that point, the format of the play on the page changes. Askari chose to write in a more traditional format where the dialogue is written all the way across the page.

Later in the play, when Warhol addresses the audience again, the format on the page shifts back to short poetic lines. Askari uses different formats to communicate how the dialogue would flow in performance.

Andy Warhol in Iran formatting looks like this:

Stage Directions: Andy enters alone, speaks directly to audience in a heightened poetic-style.

ANDY
Dialogue
Dialogue
Dialogue

Stage Directions: Farhad enters, Farhad and Andy speak in a conversational-style, Andy erects the Fourth Wall and no longer acknowledges the audience.

FARHAD
Dialogue Dialogue Dialogue Dialogue
ANDY
Dialogue Dialogue Dialogue Dialogue Dialogue Dialogue
    Dialogue Dialogue
FARHAD
Dialogue Dialogue Dialogue Dialogue Dialogue Dialogue

Overview

When you are writing pages for yourself, use whatever format you wish. If you are submitting a script for an opportunity, check and see if they have a required format.

Resources
Additional Resources

- In *Three Plays* by Christina Anderson, she uses multiple formats for each play. (Tripwire Harlot Press, 2022)
- Formatting
  - The Dramatist Guild Formatting Guide (dramatistsguild.com/script-formats)
  - The Playwright's Center Formatting Template (pwcenter.org/playwriting-toolkit/how-format-your-script)

Readings Discussed in Chapter

- *Andy Warhol in Iran* by Brent Askari (Theatrical Rights Worldwide)
- *The Antipodes* by Annie Baker (Theatre Communications Group)
- *Proof* by David Auburn (Farrar, Straus and Giroux)

Appendix B
Teaching Tools and Syllabi

As teachers, we must fit our lessons into the schedule of a larger institution. One reason I wrote the book is so that I can teach students as much as I can in the given time frame; then they can take the book home and continue working at their own pace.

Reading Aloud/Final Performances

Reading plays aloud is key to the growth of my students. Language, movement, and other theatrical elements work differently when spoken than when read silently. We read aloud to one another in class. I also encourage them to read aloud to themselves while writing and revising.

For our final class meetings, I have professional actors join us to read our plays (or sections of our plays). The students are consistently amazed by how their scripts change when spoken aloud by a professional actor and how much they learn by including actors in the process.

Contemporary Plays Come First

In the First Quarter or Semester, we only read contemporary plays (plays from the past 50 years). When I begin with older plays, it's difficult for students to penetrate the language and theatrical devices of the time, so the students end up failing to grasp the basic craft lessons that I'm teaching. By beginning with contemporary plays, they grasp the craft lessons more quickly, gain skills in reading plays more easily, and then can advance to the next level of complexity – seeing these lessons in language and history that are foreign to their everyday life.

HowlRound

HowlRound is a free national network and conversation hub for theatremakers and academics. They offer a slew of free resources, including videos, articles, syllabi support, and more: howlround.com

Sample Syllabi: Two Semesters (16 weeks each)
First Semester

In the first semester, we move through Chapters 1–20, doing writing prompts and writing a short play (10–15 pages). We also read short plays, read five full-length plays, write three short essays, and take a quiz and a test.

- Week 1: Introduction/Prologue/Chapters 1–2/ Glossary
- Week 2: Chapters 3–4, Full-length Play A.
- Week 3: Chapter 5, Full-length Play A, Quiz on Glossary Terms.
- Week 4: Chapters 6–7, Full-length Play B.
- Week 5: Chapters 8–9, Full-length Play B, Write a short essay on Play A or B.

- Week 6: Chapter 10, Full-length Play C.
- Week 7: Chapters 11–12, Full-length Play C.
- Week 8: Chapters 13–14, Full-length Play D, Write a short essay on Play C or D.
- Week 9: Chapters 15–16, Full-length Play E.
- Week 10: Chapter 17, Full-length Play E, Write a short essay on Play E.
- Week 11: Chapters 17–19, Short plays.
- Week 12: Chapter 20, Short plays.
- Week 13: Brainstorm short play ideas and pre-writing in class, read 10–15-minute plays, and write a 10–15-minute play.
- Week 14–16: Take a test on plays, write a short essay on a playwright (of your choice) and their artistic process, read aloud drafts by professional actors, submit a final draft during exams.

Second Semester

In our second semester, we write longer plays (usually 20–40-page range). We go back and use select writing prompts from the book as a springboard to write the longer play. We read/discuss two longer one-act plays and three full-length plays. We also write a reflective essay on our process.

- Week 1: Review play elements, Longer One Act #1.
- Week 2: Longer One Act #2, Pre-Writing for our own long one-act play.
- Weeks 3–5: Write/share 30 pages, Longer One Act #2.

- Weeks 6–8: Write/share/revise pages, Full-length Play F.
- Weeks 9–12: Write/share/revise pages, Full-length Plays G and H.
- Weeks 13–16: Take a test on plays, write a reflective essay on your process, read aloud drafts by professional actors, and submit a final draft during exams.

Independent Study/Workshop Option

Institutions often have an "independent study" or "workshop" option. If so, this is where my students write full-length plays.

Sample Syllabi: Quarter System

For schools with quarter systems and other short terms, I tend to focus on getting through Chapters 1–18. In general, when I work in shorter-term systems, I've happened to have students with less writing experience, so I focus on creative writing rather than both creative and analytical writing. For four short quarters in a year, the student workload looks something like this:

First Quarter

- Cover: Glossary, Chapters 1–6, Chapters 13–15.
- Write: Exercises, Scenes, and Monologues.
- Read: two full-length plays, two to three short plays.
- Quiz: On glossary terms.

Second Quarter

- Cover: Review Chapters 13–15, Chapters 7–10.
- Write: Exercises, Scenes, Monologues. (Some students who are more eager to write also write a 10–15 minute play.)
- Read: two full-length plays, two to three short plays.
- Test: On readings.

Third Quarter

Cover: Chapters 11–12, Chapters 16–18.

Write: Short play (10–15 pages).

Read: Short plays, Longer one-acts (number of readings depends on how we structure the short playwriting).

Test: On readings.

Fourth Quarter

Cover: Review Chapters 1–18 as needed, if time cover Chapters 19–25.

Write: Longer one-act (20–40 pages).

Read: Longer one-acts, full-length plays (number of readings depends on how we structure the one-act writing).

Test: On readings.

Index

357